THE NEW ENCYCLOPEDIA OF

ORIGAMI AND PAPERCRAFT TECHNIQUES

THE NEW ENCYCLOPEDIA OF
ORIGAMI AND
PAPERCRAFT TECHNIQUES

AYAKO BRODEK
EDITED BY CLAIRE WAITE BROWN

RUNNING PRESS
PHILADELPHIA · LONDON

A QUARTO BOOK

Copyright © 1991 and 2011 Quarto
Publishing Inc.

This edition published in the United States
in 2011 by Running Press Book Publishers.

9 8 7 6 5 4 3 2 1
Digit on the right indicates the number
of this printing

Library of Congress control Number:
2010925949

ISBN-13: 978-0-7624-4087-0

Conceived, designed, and produced by
Quarto Publishing Plc
The Old Brewery
6 Blundell Street
London N7 9BH

QUAR.EP02

Project editor: Chloe Todd Fordham
Art editor: Joanna Bettles
Designer: Anna Plucinska
Art Director: Caroline Guest
Picture researcher: Sarah Bell
Creative director: Moira Clinch
Publisher: Paul Carslake

Manufactured by Modern Age Pte Ltd, China
Printed by 1010 Printing International
Ltd, China

Running Press Book Publishers
2300 Chestnut Street
Philadelphia, Pennsylvania 19103-4371
Visit us on the web!
www.runningpress.com

About the New Edition by Paul Jackson   6
All About Paper   8
Paper Grain   10
Creasing and Cutting   12

UNIT 1: **ORIGAMI**   14
Origami Symbols   16
Basic Folds   18
Geometric Divisions   22
Bases   26
Decorative Designs   35
Functional Designs   38
Modular Designs   40
Action Designs   42

UNIT 2: **POP-UPS**   44
Incised Pop-ups   46
Multipiece Pop-ups   52
Boxes   56
Project: Pop-up Spider   58

UNIT 3: **PAPER SCULPTURE**   62
Cones and Cylinders   64
Decorative Forms   66
Assembly and Armatures   70
Project: Nightflight   72

UNIT 4: **BOOKBINDING**   76
Preparing the Book Block   78
Soft and Hard Covers   80
Single-section Binding   82

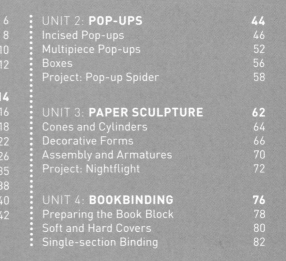

CONTENTS

Multisection Binding   85
Stab Binding   88
Project: Concertina Book   90

UNIT 5: QUILLING   **92**
Quilling Shapes   94
Quilling Applications   96
Project: Butterfly Keepsake Box   98

UNIT 6: WEAVING   **102**
Weaving Designs   104
Project: Woven Paper Bowl   108

UNIT 7: PAPER CUTTING   **112**
Paper-cutting Techniques   114
Project: Paper-cut Window Hanging   118

UNIT 8: COLLAGE   **120**
Cutting and Pasting   122
Composition   124
Project: Painted Paper Collage   126

UNIT 9: PAPIER MÂCHÉ   **128**
Casting from a Found Mold   130
Using Other Molds   132
Decorative Ideas   134

UNIT 10: PAPER PULPING   **136**
Preparing the Pulp   138
Applications   140

UNIT 11: PAPERMAKING   **142**
Making Pulp   144
Making the Paper   146
Pressing and Drying   148
Decorative Techniques   149
Papermaking Recipes   152

Index   158
Credits   160

TWO HANDS TWICE
PAUL JACKSON
These images show the two sides of
the same piece of work. A 60 x 34-in.
(150 x 86-cm) photographic print of the
artist's hands is pleated horizontally
and vertically into 96ths, and a
complex grid of small cuts made.
When the pleats were reformed, the
cuts twist parts of the image through
to the back face of the print, creating a
secondary image on the reverse. After
manipulation, the piece measures
29 x 17in. (75 x 43cm). The original
photograph is the "woven" side,
although the image is not woven, and
instead the effect is an illusion created
by the reduction of the surface when
pleated. The more abstract image
appears on the back of the "weave."
Although it uses traditional
techniques of origami and kirigami
(a variation of origami that includes
cutting), the piece is unusual
because it applies these techniques to
a visual image, rather than to a blank
sheet of paper. In that sense, the
techniques are not a means to an end,
but are used as a metaphor to
express the artist's interest in the
language of depiction.

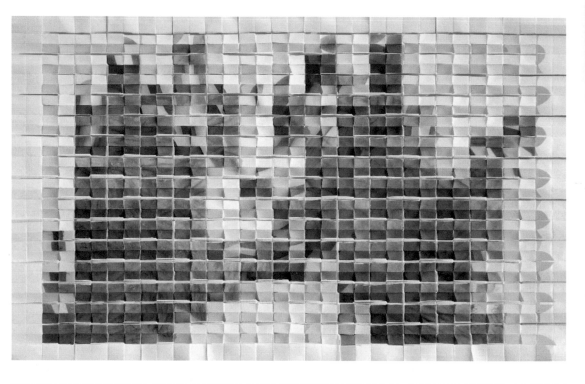

ABOUT THE NEW EDITION

In 1990–1991, I had the great pleasure to compile and write *The Encyclopedia of Origami and Papercraft*, here updated as the *The New Encyclopedia of Origami and Papercraft Techniques*. In those days, we paper artists were mostly disconnected, unknowing of each other, unorganized, considered eccentric, using a material that few outsiders considered a serious medium. The *Encyclopedia*—the first book of its kind—gave us a presence, and showed the wider world that half-hidden in ill-lit corners were people united by their love of paper, creating exceptional work in a great diversity of techniques and contexts. Perhaps more than anyone, I'm aware that the book caught the mood of the times, helping in a small way to legitimize both paper as a material, and the work created from it.

In the two decades since that original *Encyclopedia* was conceived, I would argue that paper has become the most relevant and exciting of all mediums for contemporary artists, makers, and designers. Around the world there are now frequent major exhibitions of paper art and paper is regularly seen alongside more traditional materials in even the most prestigious galleries and museums. Two decades ago, paper, other than in its traditional role as an impassive ground, was almost invisible.

What has created this change? I think it's a dizzying combination of factors, the most important of which is that because working with paper is so inherently low-tech, it puts the artist in control and so offers an antidote to today's hi-tech culture, where most of us feel we have no understanding of how things work. Paper is also cool, subversive, acceptable (now), but still slightly risky, and it offers a wide range of techniques and expression from the 3-D geometry of origami to the 2-D textured surfaces of handmade paper.

The New Encyclopedia of Origami and Papercraft Techniques combines some of the technical sections from the original book with others, and presents a completely new selection of inspirational works in paper from around the world. I hope it inspires a new generation of readers to discover the joys of paper as a creative medium, and helps to further establish paper as the most vibrant medium of our age.

Paul Jackson

ALL ABOUT PAPER

A BEWILDERING NUMBER OF PAPERS IS AVAILABLE FOR PARTICULAR USES—AND EACH TECHNIQUE IN THIS BOOK INCLUDES A SUGGESTION OF SUITABLE PAPER TYPES. HOWEVER, THE TECHNICAL SPECIFICATIONS NEED NOT NECESSARILY CONCERN THE PAPER ARTIST, TO WHOM A LOOK AND FEEL OF A PAPER IS MORE IMPORTANT. THAT SAID, KNOWLEDGE OF A FEW BASIC TYPES AND TERMS MAY PROVE USEFUL.

ORIGAMI

Origami designs can be folded using just about any paper. Traditional square papers include plain papers that are colored on one side and white on the other, and decorative "washi" papers that are durable, soft, easy to fold, and feature beautiful patterns. Scrapbooking papers are readily available in a huge range of stunning designs, and are often already square. Giftwrap also makes a feasible alternative.

Household writing or photocopy paper is perfect for practice.

POP-UPS

Pop-ups are made using thin, springy card, which can be bought in a range of colors from craft and office supply stockists. You can use medium-weight paper to work out roughs before moving on to the finished piece.

PAPER SCULPTURE

Cartridge paper is a good choice for paper sculpture, supported by a card armature as necessary. Large sculptures may benefit from a heavier paper, but this will be more difficult to manipulate. Photocopy paper is suitable for small, low-relief sculptures.

BOOKBINDING

Card-weight paper is a good choice for the pages of your book, and watercolor, handmade, and drawing papers work well. Photocopy paper is also a possibility for notebooks. Card-weight paper is also a good choice for soft covers. Hard covers made from pasteboard can be covered with papers that are thin enough to fold neatly around the corners and produce tight, crisp points and edges. Many papers are manufactured or handmade specifically for use on book covers, but it is also possible to use nonspecific papers such as giftwrap.

QUILLING
This papercraft uses strips of paper of various colors and widths that are bought specifically for the task. A widely used width is ⅛in. (3mm). Cutting your own paper is a possibility, but a time-consuming one.

WEAVING
A medium-weight paper makes a good choice for the first-time paper weaver, although papers of any weight and texture can be used to great effect as you become more experienced. Tissue papers and giftwrap, textured handmade papers, and recycled papers such as magazine pages can all be experimented with.

PAPER CUTTING
Almost any type of paper is suitable for cutting. Fine art paper is an especially good example because it cuts very neatly. Recycled and origami papers, and translucent papers, may also be used to good effect.

Handmade papers have a tendency to tear when cut, but can be used as backgrounds onto which delicately cut pieces can be mounted.

PAPER WEIGHTS

Weight is a guide to a paper's other properties and to its price. In the United States, paper weight is measured in pounds per ream (500 sheets), known as basis weight, or more often in pounds per M sheets (1,000 sheets). The size of the sheets can vary considerably from one type of paper to another, so there is no consistent relationship between the actual weight of a sheet and its official poundage. However, the most common size for measuring poundage is 25 × 38in. At this size, photocopy paper of 80gsm is 118lb, drawing paper of 150gsm is 222lb, 220gsm paper is 330lb, and so on. Tables are available to make the calculation for other sizes.

The poundage system survives outside of the United States when referring to traditional high rag papers, such as watercolor and etching papers, but for all practical purposes, conversion tables are needed whenever US poundage and paper sizes need to be converted.

In most countries outside the United States, weight is expressed in terms of the weight in grams of a sheet of paper measuring one meter square. Thus, photocopy paper is said to be 80gsm (or 80gm^2), because a 1m^2 sheet weighs 80 grams. Thinner paper, such as airmail paper, is approximately 45gsm, and thicker paper, such as cartridge drawing paper, is about 150gsm. A medium-weight card would be between 210 and 290gsm. Above 500gsm, cards are identified by thickness, measured in microns.

Some papers and cards are unusually compacted or aerated. They appear to have a high or low grammage compared to thickness, which is not necessarily a reliable indicator of weight.

COLLAGE
Collage makes use of any type of paper, whether commercial, handmade, or recycled. The only real consideration is aesthetic, and whether the various papers used work well together in the overall composition.

PAPIER MÂCHÉ
This technique traditionally uses torn-up newspaper. Large-format newspapers use paper of a better quality than tabloid newsprint, which makes it more flexible and adaptable when soaked with paste or glue. Handmade, colored, or tissue papers can also be used on the final layer to produce a decorative effect.

PAPER PULPING
Pulp can be made from any recycled paper, as long as it is neither glossy nor coated, so use newspapers, photocopy paper, leaflets, and junk mail.

PAPERMAKING
Recycled paper pulp can be made using almost any type of paper, from household writing and office paper to tissue paper, giftwrap, and junk mail. However, newspaper and glossy magazines are not a good choice, since the paper is highly acidic and the resulting sheet will quickly turn yellow and brittle.

PAPER GRAIN

ALMOST ALL CONSTRUCTION WORK WITH PAPER AND CARD MUST TAKE ACCOUNT OF THE GRAIN IN THE SHEET, AND HOW IT AFFECTS THE GENERALLY USED PAPERCRAFT TECHNIQUES OF FOLDING, TEARING, AND ROLLING.

All machine-made papers and cards have a grain, formed as the glutinous, hair-like fibers that stick together to form the sheet are vibrated to lie in line with the direction of travel of the moving belt that pulls the pulp from the "wet" end of manufacture to the "dry," gradually creating the paper. Handmade papers do not have a grain, instead the fibers lie randomly all around the sheet.

GRAIN DIRECTION

When drawing on paper, the grain is of little relevance. However, when paper is folded, rolled, torn, or cut, the influence of the fibers lying in parallel can be critical.

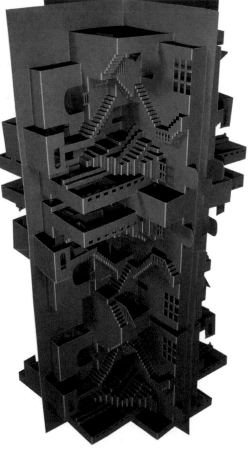

ELEVATION TERRACOTTA INGRID SILIAKUS
Paper has a character of its own that asks for cooperation. When designing a paper sculpture from scratch, the artist needs the skills of an architect to create a two-dimensional design that, with the patience and precision of a surgeon, becomes an ingenious three-dimensional wonder of paper. After the design stage, creating a paper architecture artwork requires a combination of detailed cutting and folding that takes into consideration the lie of the paper's grain.

TESTING FOR THE GRAIN

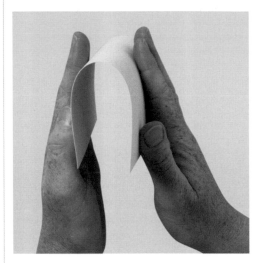

1 To find the direction of the grain, bend a sheet of paper or card in half several times, but without creasing it, to gauge the spring. Turn the sheet through 90 degrees and bring the other two edges together. A difference in tensions will be apparent. The sheet will bend more easily along the line of the fibers, or "with the grain."

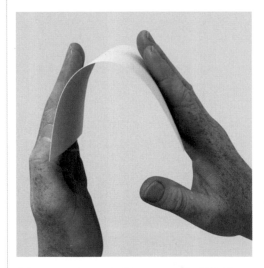

2 The paper or card will not be as flexible when bent across the line of the fibers, or "against the grain." If you have never noticed it before, this is a very surprising phenomenon.

CREASING WITH THE GRAIN

The tendency of a sheet to fold more easily when creased with the grain becomes ever more apparent if you use heavier and thicker paper. A crease made against the grain on a sheet of heavy paper or thin card will often produce a rough, broken edge at the fold. Therefore, whenever possible, crease heavier sheets with the grain, not against it.

A crease at an angle to the grain—particularly if it is one of only a few creases on the sheet—will produce unequal tensions to both sides and distort the surface of the sheet. Therefore, a shape cut out from a larger sheet may have to be oriented so that any creases on the cutout lie parallel to the grain, not at an angle to it.

The sheet has been creased against the grain, which creates a rough edge.

A crease made with the grain has a smoother edge.

TEARING WITH THE GRAIN

1 As could be predicted, a sheet will tear more cleanly with the grain than against it. Tearing with the grain gives a smooth line that follows the fibers of the paper.

2 Tearing against the grain creates a ragged effect because it breaks the fibers.

ROLLING

When rolling cylinders, the paper will roll more readily with the grain, so that tighter cylinders can be formed.

Always carry large sheets of paper or card rolled into a loose tube along the line of the grain. This will sometimes mean rolling one long edge to the opposite one to create a longer tube than may seem necessary, but the paper will be less stressed. Rolling against the grain can leave disfiguring buckle marks on the sheet. When you buy paper, always insist that heavier weights are rolled with the grain.

1 Rolling is easier with the grain, when the fibers lie along the length of the tube.

2 It can be very difficult to roll against the grain, when the fibers lie across the tube. This may even buckle the paper.

CREASING AND CUTTING

MANY PAPERCRAFT TECHNIQUES INVOLVE MAKING CREASES, WHILE GOOD CUTTING CAN MEAN THE DIFFERENCE BETWEEN A WELL-FINISHED PIECE OF WORK AND A JAGGED, UNTIDY ONE.

CREASING TECHNIQUES

Creasing is so elementary that it is frequently done without regard for the best method. One of the four methods detailed here will be ideal for any crease on any sheet. Choice depends on the weight of the sheet and the use to which the crease is being put.

CUTTING TECHNIQUES

The two tools for cutting paper and card are scissors and craft knives. Both have their merits for particular tasks, but generally you should choose whichever you feel more comfortable using. However, scissors will not cut through materials heavier than medium-weight paper and lightweight card, for which you will need to use a knife. Numerous craft or hobby knives are available, and it is advisable that you choose one with interchangeable blades.

SEE ALSO
....
Paper Grain, pages 10–11

CREASING BY HAND

Before deciding to crease by hand, crease a small piece of the sheet both with and against the grain. If the folded edges are clean and unbroken, the sheet can be creased by hand. If the folded edges are broken, the paper is too heavy to crease by hand and should be scored, cut-scored, or indented.

1 Rest the paper on a smooth, hard, level surface. Orientate the paper so that the line of the crease about to be made runs horizontally from left to right across your body. Pick up the edge or corner nearest to you and...

2 Maneuver it to the necessary position to locate the line of the crease. Hold the corner of the fold under one finger and use the finger of the other hand to make the crease. Always make sure that the crease is made at the bottom of the sheet, never down the side or across the top.

Not all creases should be made against a surface. Smaller creases, particularly in origami, are best made with the paper in the air.

SCORING

This is an easy way to crease heavy paper and light- to medium-weight card. However, scoring cuts through the surface of the sheet, so has the disadvantage of weakening it at the folded edge.

1 Place a metal ruler along the line of the crease and score with a sharp craft knife, cutting two-thirds of the way through the card. Always score on the outer, or mountain, side of a crease.

2 Bend the card backward along the score. Be aware that on coated card scoring reveals the white board beneath the color. In this instance it is better to crease by indenting.

INDENTING

This is the technique used to crease commercially manufactured cartons and boxes. The card is not weakened by scoring, but is indented under pressure along the line of the crease.

1 Indent the "wrong" side of the sheet, in this case the white side of a sheet of colored card, by turning a craft-knife blade upside down and pressing it into the card along the line of the crease. Make sure you do not break the surface of the card.

2 Bend the sheet toward you to form the crease.

3 On turning the sheet over it is clear that there is no white line and the sheet remains strong.

SAFE CUTTING

When bringing sharp knives and vulnerable fingers into close proximity, remember to always keep your free hand out of the way of the blade.

The hand that holds the sheet during cutting should never be in line with the blade.

Make sure the steadying hand is safely positioned well away from the blade.

CUT-SCORE

A technique halfway between scoring and indenting, cut-scoring should be used either for creasing very thick card or for giving thinner card a particularly flexible crease, such as might be needed on a box lid.

Using a craft knife held against a metal ruler, cut the card all the way through in a series of dashes. The length of the cuts and the distance between them depends on the thickness of the card and the degree of flexibility required, though clearly the longer the cuts, the weaker the card will be. Indent the crease for added flexibility.

CUTTING WITH SCISSORS

To make accurate cuts using scissors, keep them fixed in one hand and feed the work through them.

CUTTING WITH A KNIFE

Hold the knife like a pen for greatest control. Practice rolling the handle as you cut, so that you are not limited by the movement of your wrists when cutting a tight curve. Ensure your blade is sharp, to give a crisp edge, and use a cutting mat to save wear on the blade and damage to furniture.

**BLUE ELEPHANT
EVI BINZINGER**

Folding paper usually means dividing it into several surfaces of different sizes and forms by making straight creases. So the technique of origami itself requires the capability of abstract thinking. Inspired by nature, Evi Binzinger's models are recognizable, yet also partially abstracted. Blue Elephant is created from an uncut square of handmade washi paper, starting with a fish base and including sinks on the back, inside reverse folds for the trunk, and a little bit of molding to bring the elephant to life.

BONE FOLDER

A bone folder is not an essential tool, however it can prove to be invaluable for neatly creasing paper.

EQUIPMENT CHECKLIST

Although strictly speaking your fingers are the only essential equipment for origami, when you want to create beautiful pieces that will last, you may also find these other items useful:

• Pencil
• Craft knife
• Cutting mat
• Metal ruler
• Scissors
• Embroidery scissors (useful when making small cuts)
• Bone folder
• Glue stick

SYMBOLS

The symbols used throughout this chapter are detailed on pages 16–17.

UNIT 1
ORIGAMI

ORIGAMI IS THE BEST KNOWN OF ALL PAPERCRAFTS, PERHAPS BECAUSE IT IS THE EASIEST TO DEFINE AND BECAUSE MOST OF US HAVE DONE A LITTLE OF IT AS CHILDREN. ITS STRICT RULES PERMIT NO CUTTING, NO GLUING, AND NO DECORATION OF THE PAPER: THE SHEET MAY ONLY BE FOLDED. HOWEVER, RULES ARE THERE TO BE BROKEN, AND MANY NON-ORIGAMI PAPER ARTISTS ALSO USE BASIC FOLDING TECHNIQUES IN THEIR WORK.

**UNTITLED
MIRI GOLAN**

The way in which the origami figures have been formed from the pages of a book suggests that they are still connected to it, yet also freed from it. This piece is a rare example of origami with a message, raising global, contentious issues of conflict, reconciliation, and similarities and divides between faiths and cultures.

The blank pages of two books, handmade using thin, opaque Bible paper commonly used to make Holy books, have been carefully hollowed out so that just a frame remains, and the cutaway rectangles of each page have been divided into a square, connected to the frame by a thin strip. The squares are folded using conventional origami techniques to create kneeling figures.

BRIEF HISTORY

The history of the art of origami is somewhat obscure. The word itself is Japanese: *ori*, "to fold" and *kami*, "paper" (becoming *gami* when combined with *ori*). The name is a tribute to the ancestral home of the art, though it is a matter of dispute whether the Japanese, Koreans, or Chinese were the first to fold paper as a creative art. The Japanese developed sophisticated origami forms some 1,200 years ago, usually for symbolic or ceremonial purposes, and, contrary to subsequent rules, these were frequently cut. With the coming of Western influences in the late nineteenth century, indigenous symbolism largely disappeared, and origami became recreational. In the 1930s a young Japanese man, Akira Yoshizawa, began developing new forms from the surviving traditional ones. His single-minded dedication and creative genius helped establish origami as a creative art form.

Paper folding in the West, with the exception of a minor creative period in Spain early in the twentieth century, remained largely a schoolchild's diversion. However, in the early 1950s, a renowned British-based stage illusionist, Robert Harbin, became fascinated by the creative potential of paper folding. He collected as many traditional designs as he could (a surprising number), invented some of his own, and in 1956 published *Paper Magic*, a book that established the creative potential of the art in the West. Subsequent books by Harbin and the American paper folder Sam Randlett consolidated its position as a craft.

Since that time, in the Oriental and the Western world, tens of thousands of designs have been created in a remarkable variety of styles. Origami has an appeal possibly broader than that of any other papercraft. Many people see it as a form of puzzle-solving, an attempt to make a model from diagrams in a book with the satisfaction of having an impressive object at the conclusion. For others it is a branch of mathematics or an entertaining party trick, a vocabulary for design, or perhaps an educational aid. It is art, science, and play: recreational yet essentially profound.

PAPERS

There are no strictures regarding choice of paper. Many people like to fold with traditional square origami paper, colored on one side and white on the other, but the paper is not always easy to find. Instead, for practice, use writing or photocopy paper, and for display work experiment with as wide a range of papers as you can find. For two-tone effects use giftwrap or scrapbooking papers, which are often already square, or make your own surface with pastels, inks, or similar. Traditional Japanese paper called "washi" is durable, soft, easy to fold, and available in beautiful patterns and in small and large sizes. Some origami artists even choose to make their own papers, to ensure they get the distinct results they are looking for (see pages 142–157 for how to make your own paper).

COW
DESIGNED BY NOBORU MIYAJIMA, FOLDED BY GILAD AHARONI
When an origami design is folded to show both sides of the paper a two-colored model is created. Miyajima's cow is a complex model with many layers, and so requires a large sheet of thin, strong paper. Gilad made his paper by adhering a sheet of black Thai unryu paper to a white sheet, creating a paper that, despite its double thickness, is still quite thin and a pleasure to fold with.

AIRPLANE
HANNAH BROWN
Hannah Brown uses recycled envelopes to fold origami airplanes, making the most of the patterns on the inside of the envelope, and taking care with the folding to ensure the stamp ends up on top of the wings.

ORIGAMI SYMBOLS

SYMBOLS ARE THE CORE OF ANY DESCRIPTION OF ORIGAMI. IN RECENT DECADES, THE SYSTEM OF DIAGRAMMATIC NOTATION HAS BECOME VIRTUALLY STANDARDIZED THROUGHOUT THE WORLD, SO THAT DIAGRAMS CAN BE UNDERSTOOD WHATEVER THE LANGUAGE OF THE BOOK. SOME OF THE SYMBOLS ARE OBVIOUS, AND OTHERS WILL BE EASILY REMEMBERED WITH PRACTICE.

As you learn the basic principles of origami, refer back to these diagrams if anything seems unclear.

Direction paper moves

Fold behind

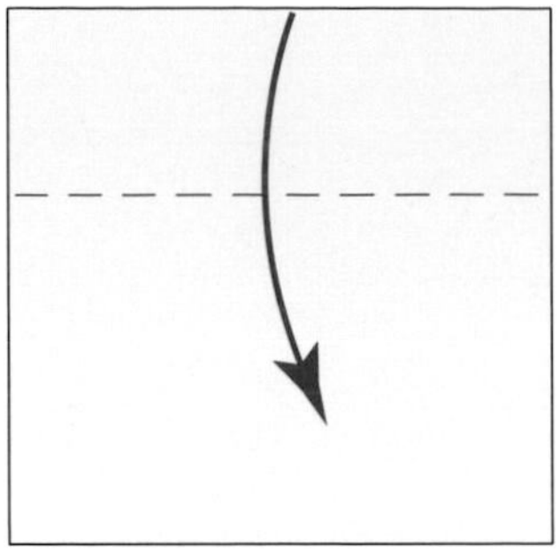

Valley fold

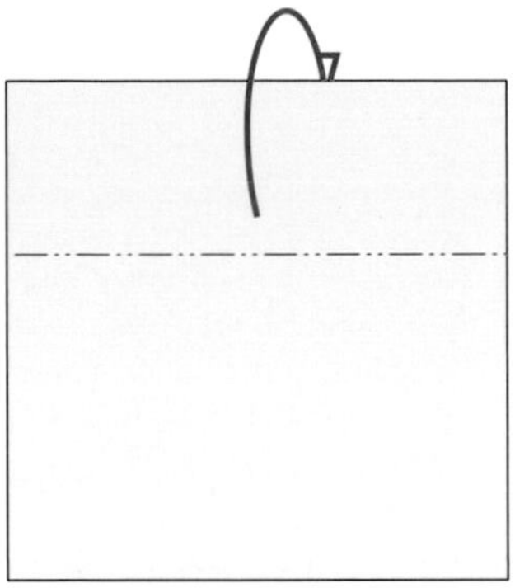

Mountain fold

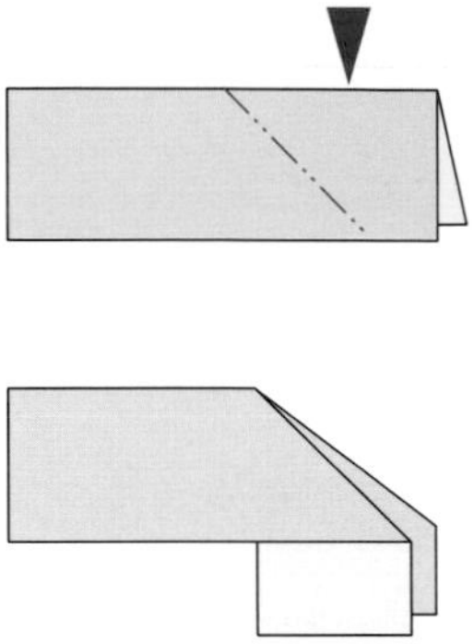

Apply pressure

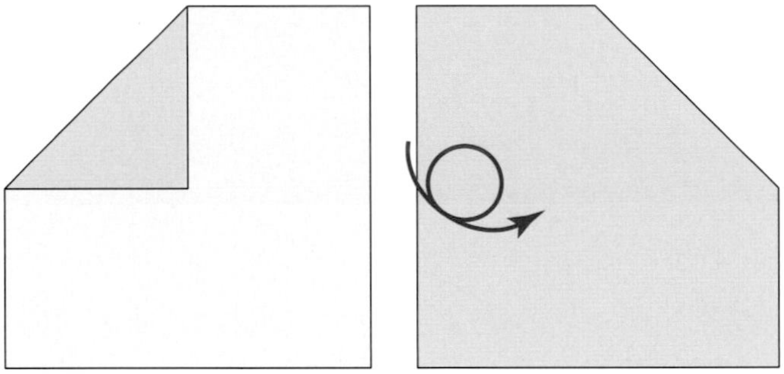

Turn over

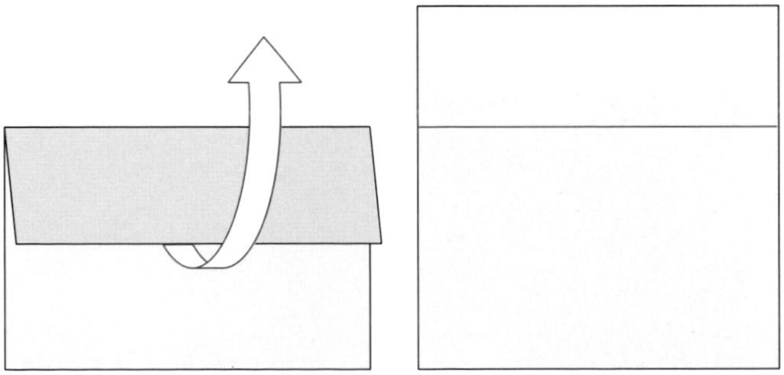

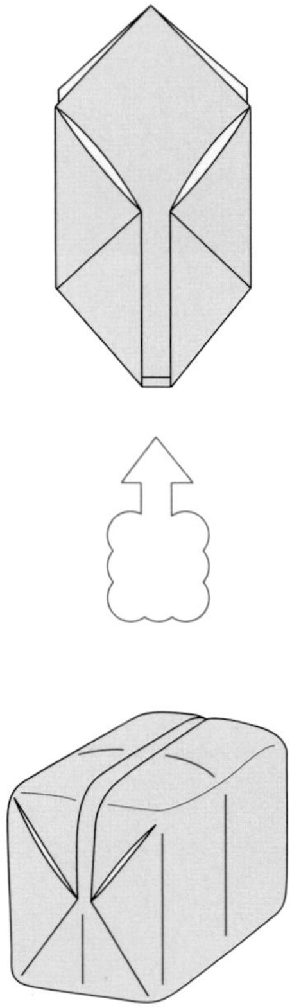

Unfold

Inflate

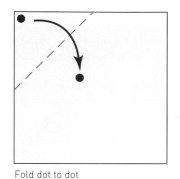

Fold dot to dot

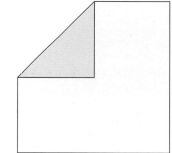

X-ray

Existing crease

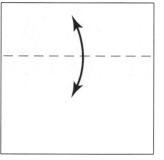

Crease and unfold

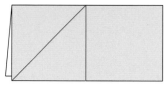
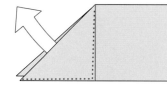

Pull out paper

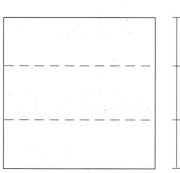

Equal distances

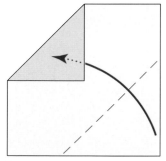

Fold under or tuck in

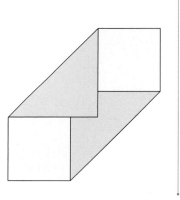

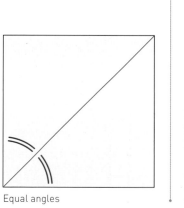

Equal angles

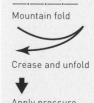

ALTERNATIVE SYMBOLS

You may also come across these symbols as variations to those listed above.

Mountain fold

Crease and unfold

Apply pressure

BASIC FOLDS

THE TECHNIQUES THAT FOLLOW FORM THE BASIS OF ORIGAMI DESIGN. HOWEVER, THEY ARE ALL SUBJECT TO AN ALMOST INFINITE RANGE OF SUBTLE INTERPRETATIONS, SO IT IS IMPORTANT TO CONCENTRATE ON THE GENERAL PRINCIPLES OF EACH TECHNIQUE AND NOT TO FEEL BOUND BY THE SPECIFIC FORMATIONS SHOWN. INDEED, THE MORE SKILLED THE ORIGAMI ARTIST BECOMES, THE MORE THE DISTINCTIONS BETWEEN TECHNIQUES BEGIN TO BLUR.

No list of techniques can be definitive— and that is part of origami's appeal. Virtually every new design can claim to introduce a fresh method, or invent a variant, subvariant, reversal, or inversion of an existing one, much as each game of chess can be said to have at least one new point of technical interest. The best way to start is to practice the techniques and become familiar with the condensed diagrammatic notations. Then, as you perfect your manipulative skill, you will also come to recognize the different techniques shown in the diagrams.

PRACTICE NOTES

When practicing your folding, work on a clean, hard, level surface. Fold with meticulous care, particularly in the early creases, since if these are incorrectly placed, every crease that follows will be out of alignment. Crease firmly. Look at one diagram and its symbols, then look ahead to the next diagram to see what the next shape will be. Never refer to one diagram in isolation.

VALLEY AND MOUNTAIN FOLDS

Valley and mountain folds are the two elementary origami creases and are the counterpart of each other: a valley is a mountain seen from the reverse side of the paper. It is a good idea to memorize the difference between the symbols for the two folds early on, so as not to confuse them.

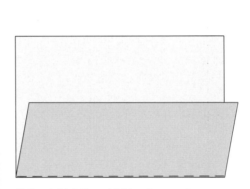

Valley fold: Lift and fold to form a sharp valley crease.

Mountain fold: Valley folds are much easier for the hands to form than mountain folds, so when a diagram indicates a mountain, it is often easier to turn the paper over and form it as a valley, then turn back to the front again. So, with the wrong side of the paper face up, lift and fold to form a sharp crease, then reverse the paper.

SQUASH FOLD

Whereas valley/mountain folds involve the formation of just one crease at a time, squash folding and other techniques involve the simultaneous formation of several creases.

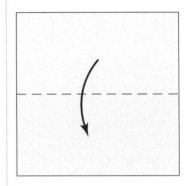

1 Fold the paper in half.

DIAGRAMMATIC NOTATION FOR SQUASH FOLD

In a diagram the squash fold would be condensed to this:

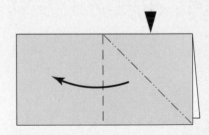

Squash

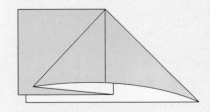

Complete

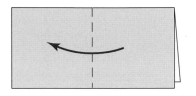

2 Fold in half again.

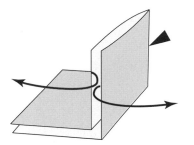

3 Loosen the opening and separate the layers apart as you apply pressure.

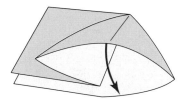

4 Squash flat. Repeating the squash fold on the other side produces the balloon base (see page 31).

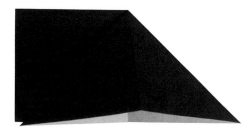

**THE COMPLETED
SQUASH FOLD**

INSIDE REVERSE FOLD

This is the most useful of all advanced origami techniques, and takes as many forms as there are designs that use it. Note that the difference between the inside reverse fold and the outside reverse fold is that, in the former, the part of the paper that moves is reversed inside the paper, and the latter is reversed outside.

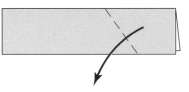

1 Fold the paper in half.

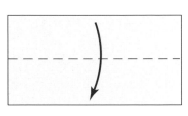

2 Make a valley fold where indicated, folding down.

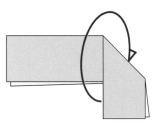

3 Refold by swiveling behind along the same crease.

DIAGRAMMATIC NOTATION FOR INSIDE REVERSE FOLD

In a diagram the inside reverse fold would be condensed to this:

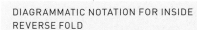

Reverse

Complete

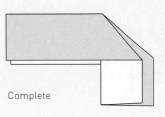

4 Unfold.

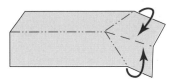

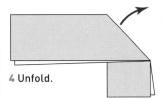

5 Form valley and mountain creases where indicated and collapse flat. Note the way in which the part of the paper strip that has been "reversed" has moved down between the layers and has turned inside out.

**THE COMPLETED
INSIDE REVERSE FOLD**

OUTSIDE REVERSE FOLD

Used less frequently than the inside reverse, this is nevertheless an important technique.

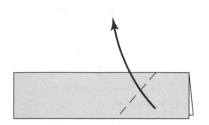

1 Fold the paper in half, then make a valley fold where indicated, folding up.

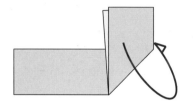

2 Refold by swiveling behind along the same crease.

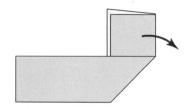

3 Unfold.

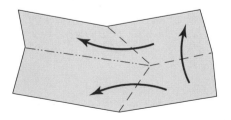

4 Form valley and mountain creases where indicated and collapse flat.

DIAGRAMMATIC NOTATION FOR OUTSIDE REVERSE FOLD

In a diagram the outside reverse fold would be condensed to this:

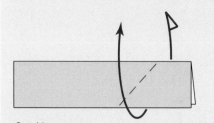

Outside reverse

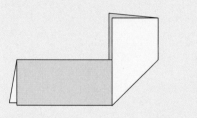

Complete

THE COMPLETED OUTSIDE REVERSE FOLD

RABBIT EAR FOLD

The technique is so-called because the free point resembles a rabbit's ear. In a subsequent maneuver, that point is frequently stood upright and squashed.

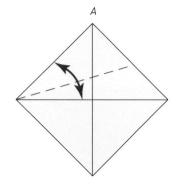

1 Crease and unfold on both diagonals. Fold the top left edge to the horizontal creased line and unfold.

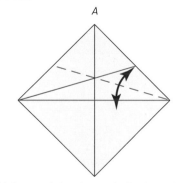

2 Fold the top right edge to the horizontal ceased line and unfold.

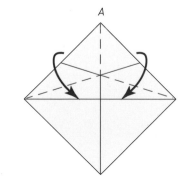

3 Now fold both sides together to the horizontal creased line, lifting point A and forming a rabbit ear.

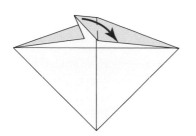

4 Flatten the ear to one side.

THE COMPLETED RABBIT EAR FOLD
Repeating the folds on the lower half of the sheet is an alternative method of making the fish base (see page 34).

DIAGRAMMATIC NOTATION FOR RABBIT EAR FOLD

In a diagram the rabbit ear fold would be condensed to this:

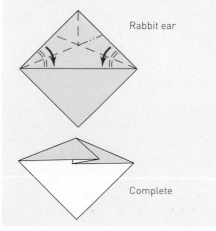

Rabbit ear

Complete

SINK FOLD
This is perhaps one of the most complex origami techniques, primarily because of the large number of creases that have to be simultaneously manipulated.

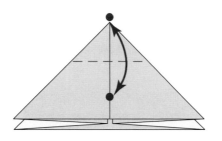

1 Start with a balloon base (see page 31). Fold dot to dot to crease where the "sink line" will be, then unfold.

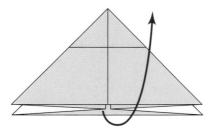

2 Unfold the paper completely.

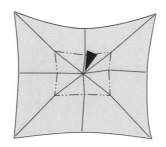

3 Crease mountains around the center square, pushing the center down into the paper.

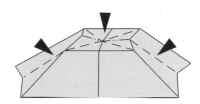

4 Collapse flat pushing from both sides.

THE COMPLETED SINK FOLD
In origami any "closed" point may be inverted and sunk (or multisunk in a series of concentric sinks). The technique is a useful way to create long, free points.

DIAGRAMMATIC NOTATION FOR SINK FOLD:

In a diagram the sink fold would be condensed to this:

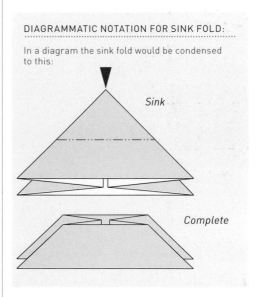

Sink

Complete

SEE ALSO
Origami Symbols, pages 16–17

GEOMETRIC DIVISIONS

HIDDEN WITHIN ALL ORIGAMI DESIGNS IS A PATTERN OF GEOMETRIC CREASES. MOST CREASE PATTERNS FOLLOW SIMPLE SYSTEMS, SUCH AS DIVIDING AN EDGE OR ANGLE INTO HALVES OR QUARTERS. HOWEVER, THERE ARE OTHER SYSTEMS THAT ARE MORE SOPHISTICATED. THESE SEPARATE INTO TWO CATEGORIES: EDGE OR ANGLE DIVISION; AND THE FOLDING OF POLYGONS—REGULAR-SIDED SHAPES, SUCH AS A HEXAGON OR OCTAGON.

No division relies on guesswork or trial and error: each is made by folding one specific point to another, and each can be proved accurate using geometric or trigonometric theorems. They are all quick and reliable, and do not require the use of a protractor, compass, ruler, or pencil. More important, they are all supremely elegant.

Surprisingly, there is not just one way to fold a polygon, but many. Some methods are direct, while others are more complex, revealing unexpected and satisfying edge or crease alignments during the construction.

BEAK

This humorous design, in which the mouth opens and closes, is made by dividing the edge into thirds. Origami purists would regard the drawn eyes as a cheat, arguing that eyes could be achieved by folding. They are correct!

EDGE DIVISION

To create thirds along an edge, follow this simple method.

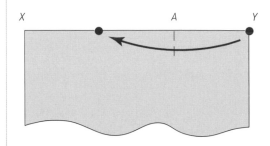

1 Fold Y toward X, estimating one-third. Pinch the paper at A.

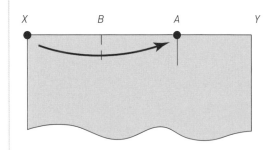

2 Fold X to pinch A, pinching at B.

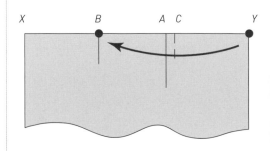

3 Fold Y to B, pinching at C (near A).

SEE ALSO
Origami Symbols, pages 16–17

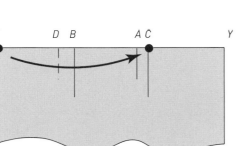

4 Fold X to C, pinching at D (near B). Repeat, folding Y, then X, then Y, then X, etc. across to the last pinch made, until a pinch is made on top of an existing pinch. That is a perfect third of edge XY.

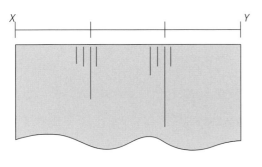

5 Similar systems, but with different XY folding patterns can be devised to fold any division.

ANGLE DIVISION
This method to divide any angle into thirds is closely related to the edge division technique.

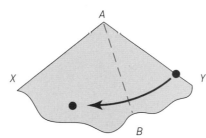

1 Angle XAY is arbitrary. Fold AY toward AX, estimating one-third. Crease AB.

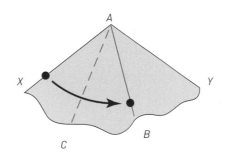

2 Fold AX to AB, creasing AC.

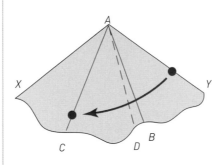

3 Fold AY to AC, creasing AD (near AB).

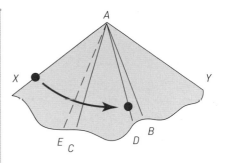

4 Fold AX to AD, creasing AE (near AC). Repeat, folding AY to AE, then folding AX to that crease, then AY to this new crease, and so on, until a crease is made on top of an existing crease. That is a perfect third of angle XAY.

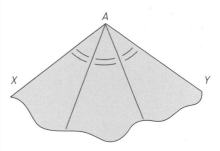

5 Similar systems, but with different AX–AY folding patterns can be devised to fold any angle into any number of equal angles.

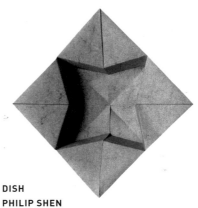

DISH
PHILIP SHEN
The form of this shallow dish by Philip Shen is achieved by angle division, dividing the corners of a square into equal thirds. A further set of creases is then added and the form collapsed into shape.

POLYGONS: EQUILATERAL TRIANGLE
Use a rectangle of paper.

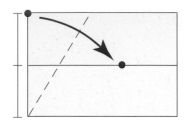

1 Precrease the midpoint horizontal, then fold dot to dot.

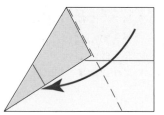

2 Fold across.

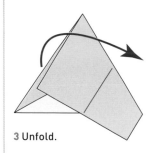

3 Unfold.

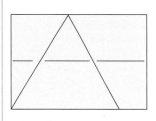

4 Cut off the excess paper.

THE COMPLETED EQUILATERAL TRIANGLE
If the crease that is formed when creating a triangle is considered to scar the design, it may be largely eliminated by creasing only at the Step 1 location point, not along the whole length of the paper.

POLYGONS: HEXAGON
Use a square of paper.

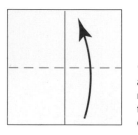

1 Precrease a vertical midpoint, then fold the bottom edge to the top.

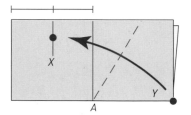

2 Pinch the three-quarter crease X. Fold corner Y to touch crease X, so that this new crease starts exactly at A.

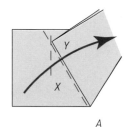

3 Fold the other edge across.

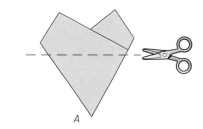

4 Cut off the excess paper and open the triangle into a hexagon.

THE COMPLETED HEXAGON
The hexagon will be misproportioned if the cut at Step 4 is incorrectly made, so make it with care. The creases are usefully placed and should not spoil a design.

POLYGONS: OCTAGON
Begin with a square of paper.

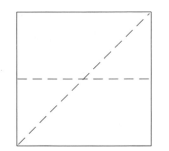

1 Precrease one diagonal and the horizontal.

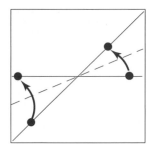

2 Align these two creases.

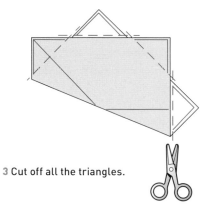

3 Cut off all the triangles.

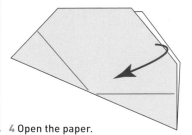

4 Open the paper.

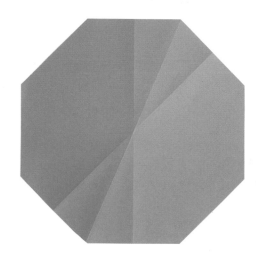

THE COMPLETED OCTAGON
This is a very elegant and accurate way to fold an octagon, because the paper never becomes bulky and the triangles are easy to cut off.

IRISES
These designs have been folded from an equilateral triangle, a hexagon, and an octagon, to make blooms with three, six, or eight petals. They are all made in exactly the same way as the traditional four-petal iris folded from a square (see Flower Base, page 30). It is clear that the greater the number of edges that a polygon has, the shorter the petals become. This interesting exercise can be performed on most geometric designs.

BASES

A NUMBER OF ORIGAMI DESIGNS START LIFE AS A PARTICULAR SEQUENCE OF FOLDS, KNOWN AS A "BASE," AND A THOROUGH KNOWLEDGE OF SOME OF THESE SEQUENCES WILL ENABLE YOU TO GO ON AND PRODUCE A WIDE RANGE OF ORIGAMI SHAPES.

When origami began to be analyzed in the early part of the last century, it came to light that several designs began with an identical sequence of folds. These came to be known as "bases," and were given names that often reflected a design common to them.

ROCK CRAB
MARC KIRSCHENBAUM

Marc Kirschenbaum's rock crab is heavy on appendages, and is folded using two sheets of mulberry bark paper bonded onto aluminum foil—the foil backing means the model is able to maintain its shape. The crab's structure is rooted in the traditional balloon base, with the five flaps of this base further split into more flaps through specialized folding sequences. The top thick tip is split into two, and the resulting flaps formed into the back legs, while splitting two of the larger flaps into three forms the remaining legs. The remaining two large flaps become the claws.

KITE BASE

Also known as the "ice-cream cone" base, the kite is one of the simplest origami bases. The name derives from its kite-like shape, equally you might see it as an ice-cream cone.

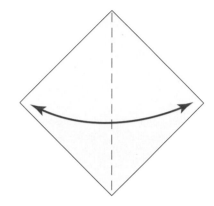

1 Hold the paper at an angle so you are looking at a diamond shape. Fold the paper in half widthwise and unfold.

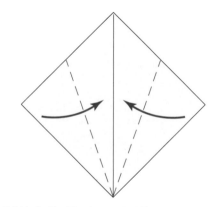

2 Fold in both sides to meet at the crease.

THE COMPLETED
KITE BASE

SEE ALSO
....
Origami Symbols, pages 16–17
Basic Folds, pages 18–21

BLINTZ BASE

The word blintz comes from a way of folding pastry. In Japan, it is called *zabuton*, meaning "cushion," from a way of sewing fabric together to make a *zabuton*.

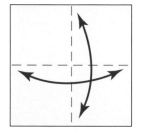

1 Fold the paper in half lengthwise and unfold. Then fold it in half widthwise and unfold.

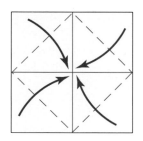

2 Fold the four corners into the center.

THE COMPLETED BLINTZ BASE

OTHER SIMPLE BASES

These simple folds may be referred to as "book" and "cupboard" bases.

BOOK BASE   **CUPBOARD BASE**

PRELIMINARY BASE

Traditionally, many origami bases were given names that reflected a design common to them, such as bird or flower. However, the preliminary base does not follow this tradition, and is so-called because it is the starting point for many different designs. There are two methods of forming this base.

METHOD A

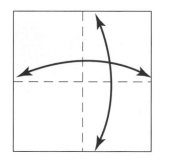

1 Fold the paper in half lengthwise and unfold. Then fold it in half widthwise and unfold.

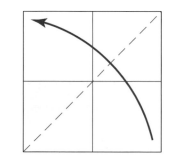

2 Fold in half diagonally.

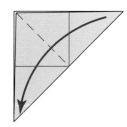

3 Fold the triangle in half.

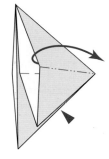

4 Open up the top triangle and squash it to form a square.

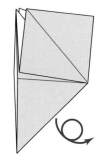

5 Turn the piece over.

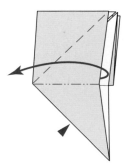

6 Repeat Step 4 on the other side.

THE COMPLETED PRELIMINARY BASE

METHOD B

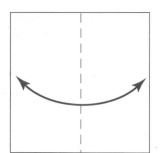

1 Fold the paper in half widthwise and unfold.

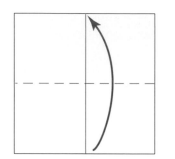

2 Fold it in half lengthwise from bottom to top.

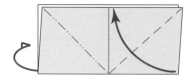

3 Fold the bottom right corner to the top center, and mountain fold the bottom left corner to the top center.

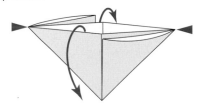

4 Open up the center layers and press the sides together, then flatten the piece in half. When moving on from this point, ensure the base is facing in the right direction at each subsequent stage of folding.

THE COMPLETED PRELIMINARY BASE

**BARREL CACTUS
JOHN BLACKMAN**

Blackman's cactus is based on a traditional Japanese decoration called a *kusadama*. The 36 cactus elements—each one made from one square of paper—the three flowers—each constructed using three squares of paper—and the pot all begin with preliminary bases. The bases for the cactus elements are folded into a flat model, unfolded, and refolded inside out to create the three-dimensional element.

BIRD BASE

The bird base is also sometimes referred to as the crane base, not surprisingly because it forms the basis of the popular crane pattern.

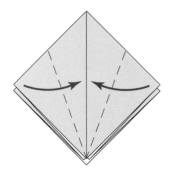

1 Begin with a preliminary base, positioned with the open corners down. Fold the right and left edges of the top layer flaps to meet at the center.

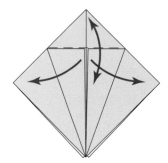

2 Fold the top triangle down and unfold, then unfold the folds made in Step 1.

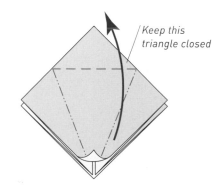

Keep this triangle closed

3 Lift the bottom point of the top layer and swing it upward, keeping the top triangle closed.

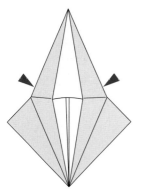

4 Push the left and right corners toward each other, so that both edges meet at the center. Press flat.

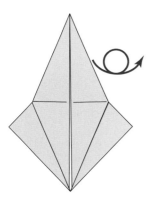

5 Turn the piece over. Repeat Steps 1 to 4 on the other side.

THE COMPLETED BIRD BASE

FOLDING A CRANE FROM A BIRD BASE

These flaps become wings

These flaps separate in the middle

1 Begin with a bird base, positioned with the wing sides up. Fold the right and left lower edges of the top layer to meet at the center. Turn the piece over and repeat this step on the other side.

2 Make inside reverse folds (see page 19) on both sides.

3 To form the crane's beak, make an inside reverse fold on one end. Pull the wings apart to complete the crane.

THE COMPLETED CRANES

FLOWER BASE

Flowers of various varieties are popular origami designs, and many begin with the flower base.

1 Begin with a preliminary base, positioned with the open corners down. Fold the right upper edge of the top layer to align with the center line, then unfold.

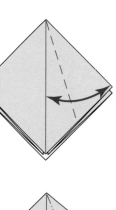

2 Loosen an opening in the top right, and fold to the left, forming a diamond shape.

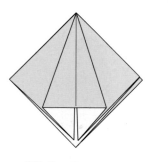

3 Flatten the diamond and press down firmly. Repeat Steps 1 and 2 on the remaining three faces.

THE COMPLETED FLOWER BASE

MAKING AN IRIS FROM A FLOWER BASE

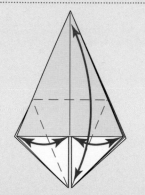

1 Begin with a flower base. Fold it in half lengthwise and unfold. Fold the right and left bottom edges of the top layer to meet at the center, then unfold.

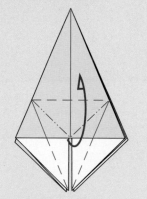

2 Lift up the bottom of the triangle and loosen an opening.

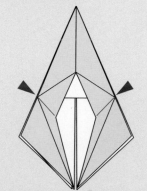

3 Push the right and left corners inward to meet at the center, then flatten.

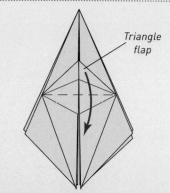

Triangle flap

4 Fold down the triangle flaps. Repeat Steps 1 to 4 on the remaining three faces.

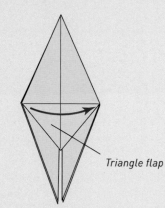

Triangle flap

5 Fold one flap to the side to show the face without a triangle flap.

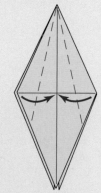

6 Fold the right and left lower edges of the top layer to meet at the center.

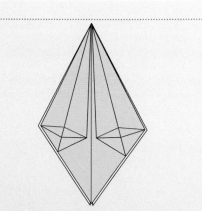

7 Repeat Steps 5 and 6 on the remaining three faces.

8 Open all four petals.

THE COMPLETED IRIS

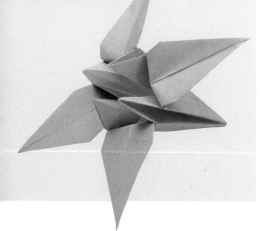

BALLOON BASE

Some call this the "water bomb" base, because once you make a balloon from it you can actually put water in it. The crease pattern of this base is the same as for the preliminary base. You can take a preliminary base and flip it around to form a balloon base.

1 Fold the paper in half diagonally and unfold. Then fold in half diagonally in the other direction and unfold.

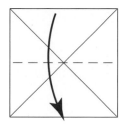

2 Fold in half lengthwise.

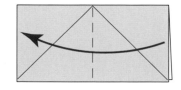

3 Fold in half widthwise.

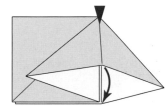

4 Loosen the opening and separate the layers as you apply pressure.

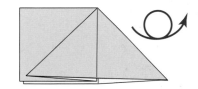

5 Squash the open square to form a triangle.

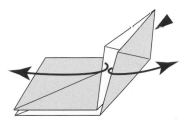

6 Turn the piece over and repeat Steps 4 and 5 on the other side.

THE COMPLETED BALLOON BASE

MAKING A BALLOON FROM BALLOON BASE

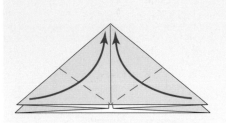

1 Begin with a balloon base. Fold the two bottom corners of the top layer to meet at the top corner point.

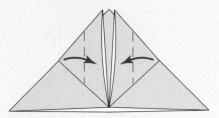

2 Fold both right and left corners of the top layer to meet at the center.

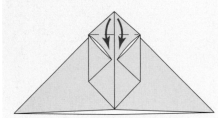

3 Fold the top triangle flaps in half.

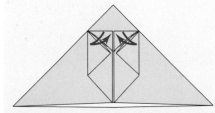

4 Fold the triangles down, then unfold them.

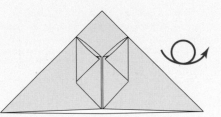

Pocket ——————   —————— Pocket

5 Loosen the pockets and insert the triangles in the pockets.

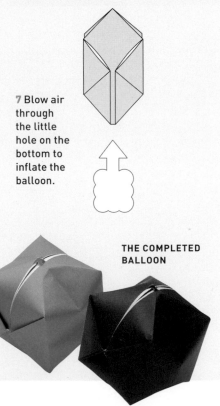

6 Turn the piece over and repeat Steps 1 to 5 on the other side.

7 Blow air through the little hole on the bottom to inflate the balloon.

THE COMPLETED BALLOON

BOAT BASE

This base has lots of different names, including the "windmill" base because of its shape, the "pig" base because it can be made into a pig, and also the "multiform" base.

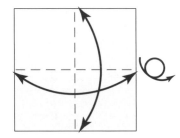

1 Fold the paper in half lengthwise and unfold. Then fold it in half widthwise and unfold. Turn the piece over.

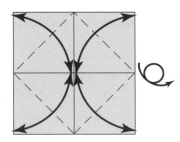

2 Fold the four corners to the center then unfold. Turn the piece over.

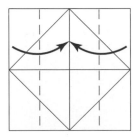

3 Fold both sides to meet at the center crease.

4 Fold the top and bottom edges to meet at the center crease.

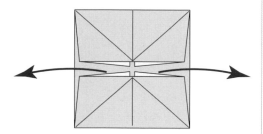

5 Pinch the inner corners of the bottom portion from the center and pull them outward.

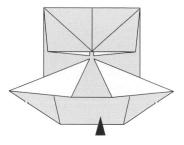

6 Flatten the bottom. Repeat Step 5 on the top portion.

THE COMPLETED BOAT BASE

ALTERNATIVE NAMES
You can see from these examples of what the boat base can be made into, why it is also known as a "windmill," "pig," or "double-boat" base.

MAKING A SAILBOAT FROM A BOAT BASE

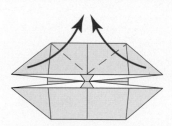

1 Begin with the boat base and fold up the two triangle flaps on the top portion.

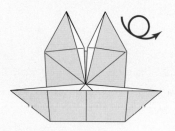

2 Turn the piece over.

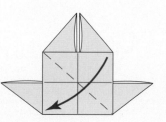

3 Fold the square part in half diagonally.

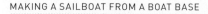

THE COMPLETED SAILBOAT

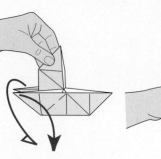

TRICKY BOAT
This sailboat is known in Japan as *damashi-bune*, meaning "tricky boat." Ask a friend to hold the sail tight without letting go, then ask them to close their eyes. While they cannot see, fold down the two flaps next to the sail, then tell them to open their eyes. It appears as if they let go of the sail and the boat is sinking.

FISH BASE

The fish base is an extension of the rabbit ear fold (see page 20), and the "rabbit ears" can also be folded to form the fins of various sea creatures.

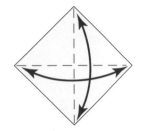

1 Place the paper at an angle so you are looking at a diamond shape. Fold the paper in half widthwise and unfold. Then fold it in half lengthwise and unfold.

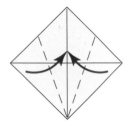

2 Fold both sides to meet at the center crease.

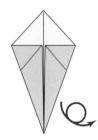

3 Turn the piece over.

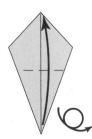

4 Fold in half lengthwise, then turn the whole piece over.

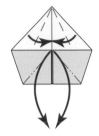

5 Fold the right-side edge to meet the center crease, at the same time pulling down the right-side inner corner to form a point. Repeat on the left side.

6 Fold down the top layer.

7 Turn the piece over.

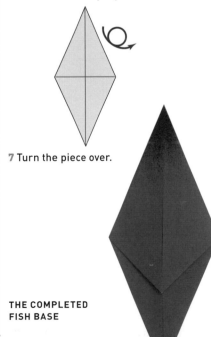

THE COMPLETED FISH BASE

MAKING A FISH FROM A FISH BASE

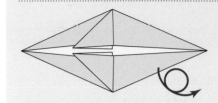

1 Begin with a fish base, positioning it sideways. Turn the piece over, keeping the small triangular flaps on the left side.

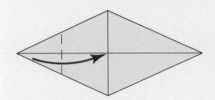

2 Fold the left corner to the center.

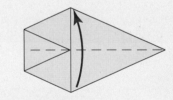

3 Fold in half lengthwise.

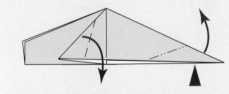

4 Fold down the small triangular flaps diagonally to form fish fins. Repeat on the other side. To form the fish's tail, make an inside reverse fold (see page 19) on the other end.

THE COMPLETED FISH

DECORATIVE DESIGNS

IT IS ONE THING TO UNDERSTAND THE TECHNIQUES OF PAPER FOLDING, BUT TECHNIQUES BY THEMSELVES MEAN LITTLE. IN ORIGAMI, MORE THAN IN ANY OTHER PAPERCRAFT, IT IS IMPORTANT TO SEE HOW THE TECHNIQUES RELATE TO SPECIFIC DESIGNS.

CREATING A LIKENESS

Ornamental models, such as representations of animals or flowers, can be simple or complex, requiring practice and patience. In drawing, the likeness of a subject may be rendered with just a few skilled strokes of a pen. So it is with origami, but using folds. It is a demanding, creative challenge to reduce a complex shape to its essential form, then to fold that form in a simple and elegant manner.

SEE ALSO
Origami Symbols, pages 16–17
Basic Folds, pages 18–21
Bases, pages 26–34

BUTTERFLY
This butterfly is a suitable project for those new to origami.

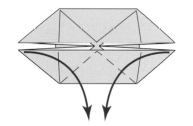

1 Begin with a boat base (see pages 32–33). Fold down the two bottom triangle flaps.

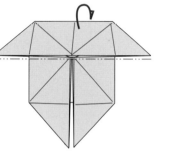

2 Mountain fold the top portion.

3 Fold both corners at a slight angle, as shown.

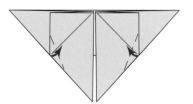

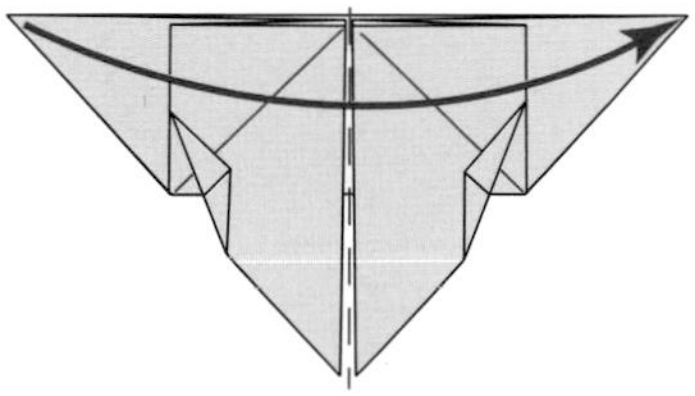

4 Fold in half widthwise.

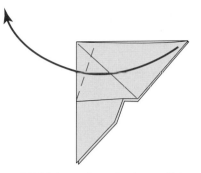

5 Fold the top layer back at a slight angle, as shown.

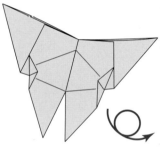

6 Turn the piece over.

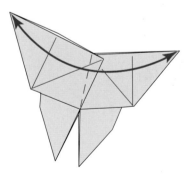

7 Fold in half, aligning the wings, then unfold.

THE COMPLETED BUTTERFLIES

SNAIL
Ayako Brodek's snail design is a variation of a traditional model, and one that is more suited to the intermediate origamist.

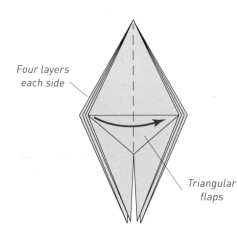

Four layers each side

Triangular flaps

1 Follow Steps 1 to 4 of Making an Iris from a Flower Base (see page 30). Position the piece with the same number of layers on both right and left sides. Make sure the triangular flaps are all down. Fold one left layer to the right side to show the face without a triangular flap.

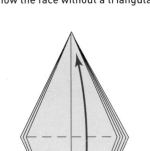

2 Bring the bottom corner of the top layer all the way to the top corner.

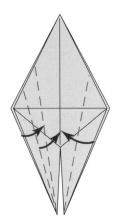

3 Turn the piece over.

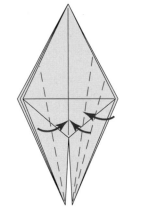

4 Take two layers of the right-side lower edges, and fold them two-thirds of the way to the center, then fold again to meet the center. Take one layer of the left-side lower edge, and fold it to meet the center.

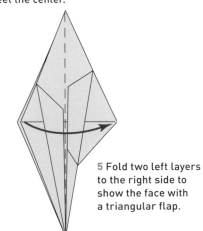

5 Fold two left layers to the right side to show the face with a triangular flap.

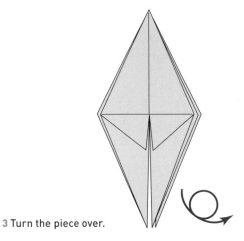

6 Take two layers of the left-side lower edges and fold them two-thirds of the way to the center, then fold again to meet the center. Take one layer of the right-side lower edge and fold it to meet the center.

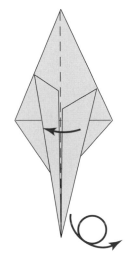

7 Fold one right layer to the left side to show the face without a triangular flap. Then turn the piece over.

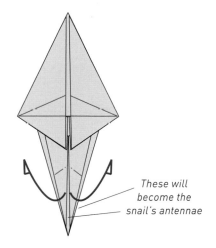

8 Mountain fold the antennae at a slight angle.

These will become the snail's antennae

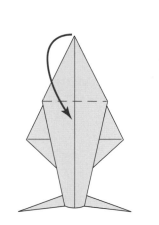

10 Fold up the top triangle, leaving one layer behind. Stand the triangle up.

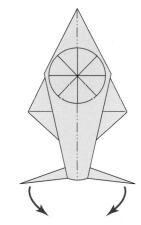

12 To form the snail, mountain fold the center of the body and tail by pinching them, and fold up the antennae.

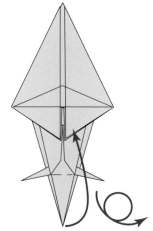

9 Fold the bottom corner up and tuck it underneath the triangular flap. Then turn the piece over.

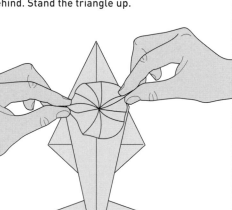

11 Carefully pull open all folds of the triangle to form the snail's shell.

THE COMPLETED SNAILS

FUNCTIONAL DESIGNS

WHILE YOU MAY THINK IMMEDIATELY OF ORIGAMI DESIGNS AS MERELY DECORATIVE, THERE ARE A SURPRISING NUMBER OF FUNCTIONAL DESIGNS.

Boxes are the most popular subject, some simple, others very elaborate. Turned upside down, many boxes make excellent hats. Other origami items to wear include warm newspaper slippers, modular belts, and all kinds of jewelry.

ORIGAMI IN THE HOME

In the kitchen, simple leakproof cups, saucers, or boxes can be folded from aluminum foil or wax paper. On the dining table, decoratively folded paper or linen napkins are often seen, and origami can be used to make place cards, napkin rings, and takeaway bags. So, while paper-folded objects may not have a major everyday role, they can be useful as well as attractive.

SEE ALSO
Origami Symbols, pages 16–17
Basic Folds, pages 18–21
Bases, pages 26–34

TABLE DECORATIONS

The egg stand can be softened slightly by rolling the tip of each square flap around a pencil. The stand is used here as a table decoration, to display a plastic egg that has been decorated with torn and cut paper. How to make the butterfly on top is detailed on page 35.

1 Begin with a blintz base (see page 27). Fold this base into a boat base (page 32), using this side as the colored (right) side of the paper, which means you need to turn the piece over to carry out Step 1 of the boat base.

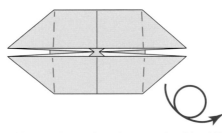

2 Now you have a boat base, made with a blintz base. Turn the piece over.

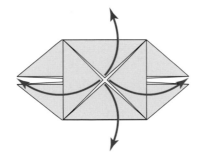

3 Unfold the four triangular flaps, bringing all four inner corners out.

4 Turn the piece over.

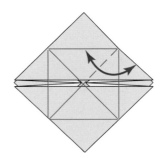

5 Fold one triangular flap back and forth, so that it stands up.

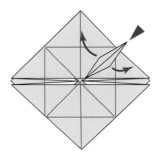

6 Loosen the opening and squash to form a square.

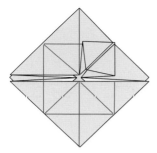

7 Repeat Steps 5 and 6 on the remaining three flaps, to give four squares that each look like a preliminary base.

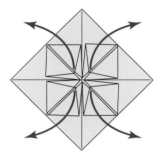

8 Pull all four square flaps out a little to make space for an egg in the center.

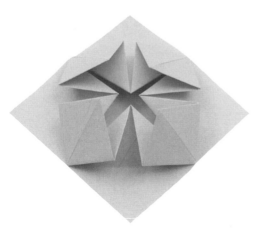

THE COMPLETED EGG STAND

PICTURE FRAME
By adding more folds, you can turn the egg stand into a picture frame.

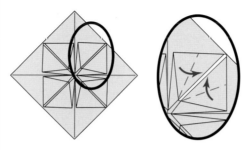

1 Fold until Step 7 of the egg stand. Working on one of the four squares in the center of the piece, fold both right and left lower edges to meet the center. Repeat on the remaining three squares.

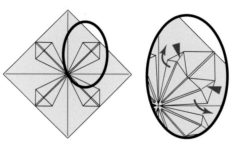

2 Bringing back the top layer of each side, loosen an opening and squash flat. Do the same on the remaining three squares.

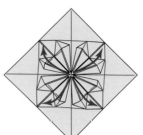

3 Fold all four inner pointy corners outward.

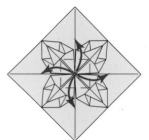

4 Fold all four inner points outward.

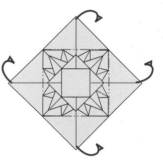

5 Mountain fold all four triangular flaps. Use the side triangular flaps to make the frame freestanding.

THE COMPLETED PICTURE FRAME
Origami picture frames show off other origami creations beautifully.

MODULAR DESIGNS

MODULAR FOLDING IS A PARTICULAR GENRE OF ORIGAMI IN WHICH IDENTICALLY FOLDED UNITS LOCK TOGETHER WITHOUT GLUE TO CREATE LARGER SHAPES.

SEE ALSO
Origami Symbols, pages 16–17
Basic Folds, pages 18–21
Bases, pages 26–34

The appeal of modular work is a satisfying mix of geometry, color patterns, and simple folding. There is also a strong sense of the whole being more than the parts, of a spectacular structure made with little effort.

Each module is folded from one sheet of paper and the units are fitted together by inserting flaps into pockets created by the folding process, in a technique that allows the origamist to create larger and more complex designs than would be possible with a single sheet of paper.

STELLA
MEENAKSHI MUKERJI
This model belongs to a series named Enhanced Sonobes. The Sonobe Unit, invented by Mitsunobu Sonobe in the 1970s, is one of the foundations of modular origami. Stella is about 6in. (15cm) in diameter and is made up of 30 units locked together in a dodecahedral/icosahedral symmetry that start with rectangles. The units are interlocked together without the help of glue.

FIVE-MODULE ANTIPRISMS
The modules in the model shown here, designed by Miyuki Kawamura for her book *Polyhedron Origami for Beginners*, fit neatly together by means of a flap that inserts into a pocket on the adjacent module.

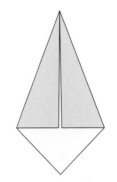

1 Begin with a kite base (see page 26), positioned upside down.

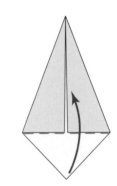

2 Bring the bottom triangle up, folding along the bottom edge of the top triangle.

USES AND VARIATIONS
This model can be used as a holder for a battery operated candle, and by curving or pleating the top of the triangle flaps, you can make it more decorative.

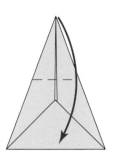

3 Fold in half lengthwise, bringing the top corner to the bottom.

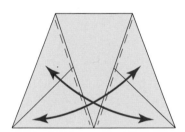

4 Fold both sides along the edges of the top layer triangle, then unfold leaving firm crease lines.

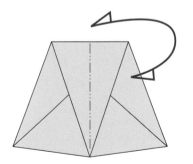

5 Mountain fold in half widthwise, then unfold leaving a firm crease line.

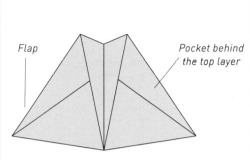

Flap   *Pocket behind the top layer*

6 The finished module. Each module has a flap and pocket. Make four more modules using paper of the same size.

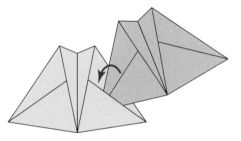

7 Insert a flap of one module into the pocket of another module.

THE COMPLETED ARRANGEMENT OF ANTIPRISMS

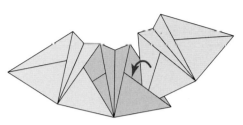

8 Add three more modules by inserting the flaps into the pockets.

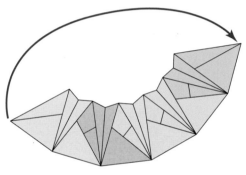

9 Insert the flap of the first module into the pocket of the fifth module to complete the antiprism.

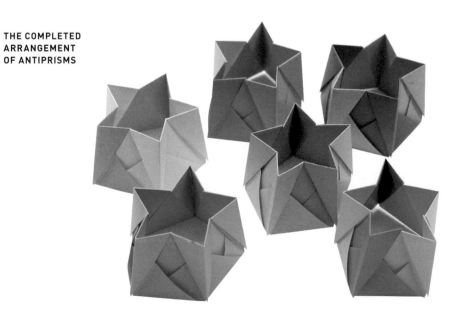

ACTION DESIGNS

ACTION MODELS ARE DESIGNS TO BE PLAYED WITH. HOWEVER, THAT DOES NOT MEAN THIS GENRE OF ORIGAMI SHOULD BE CONFINED TO THE CLASSROOM.

At their best, action models are the most easily appreciated, most original, most ingeniously designed, and most entertaining of all origami designs. They are neither childish nor banal. A design that jumps, spins, flaps, winks, tumbles, talks, balances, makes a noise, or flies is easy to admire and enjoy.

POPULAR CHOICES

The traditional Japanese flapping bird, with wings that move when its tail is pulled, has been known in the West since the 1860s, and is possibly the finest of all origami designs. The hungry crow is also a good, traditional example of an action model.

SEE ALSO

Origami Symbols, pages 16–17
Basic Folds, pages 18–21
Bases, pages 26–34

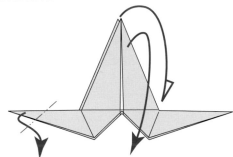

THE COMPLETED FLAPPING BIRD

FLAPPING BIRD
This traditional model is a classic design.

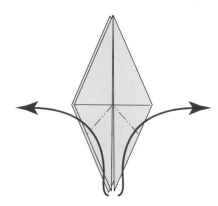

1 Begin with a bird base (see pages 28–29). Make inside reverse folds (see page 19) on both sides.

2 To form the bird's beak, make an inside reverse fold on one end. Pull the wings apart.

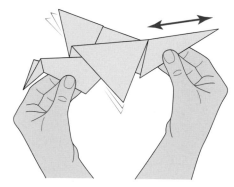

GET FLAPPING
To flap the bird's wings, hold its breast and gently move its tail.

HUNGRY CROW

This is another traditional model that can be very entertaining.

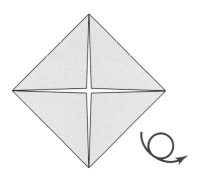

1 Begin with a blintz base (see page 27). Turn the piece over.

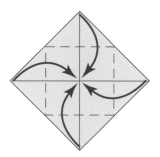

2 Fold the four corners to the center.

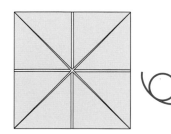

3 Turn the piece over.

4 Fold a balloon base (page 31), using this side as the white (back) side of the paper.

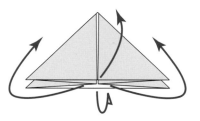

5 Unfold the balloon base and face the side with four square flaps (the same side as shown in Step 4). Position it diagonally.

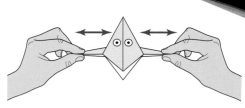

EAT UP

To make the hungry crow eat, hold the wings and pull them back and forth sideways to make the mouth open and close. The crow can actually grab small things with his mouth.

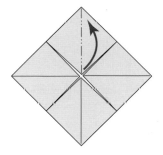

6 Lift the inner corner of the top square, loosen the opening, and crease the center by mountain folding.

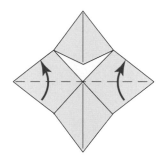

7 Fold in half horizontally both right and left squares.

THE COMPLETED HUNGRY CROW

CARD
Thin card suitable for making finished pop-ups is available from craft and office supply stores in a range of colors. Squares of thin card are used in scrapbooking and cardmaking, and can be bought from craft suppliers in packs containing various colors and decorative patterns.

UNIT 2
POP-UPS

USING CUTS, FOLDS, AND SOMETIMES ADD-ON PIECES, POP-UPS TRANSFORM A SHEET OF CARD FROM TWO DIMENSIONS TO THREE AND BACK AGAIN. IT IS EASY TO SEE WHY THEY HAVE SUCH AN ENDURING FASCINATION, SINCE THEY ARE OFTEN EXTRAORDINARILY INGENIOUS, COMBINING THE RIGORS OF GEOMETRY WITH THE APPEAL OF MAGIC.

BOOK
PAUL JOHNSON
This is a multi-piece pop-up, using techniques derived from incised generations techniques.

SEED IN THE WIND
JEMMA WESTING
This multipiece pop-up is the result of a brainstorming exercise by the artist, who considered the journey of a seed through the air, traveling through wind tunnels, turbulence, and thermals in the sky. It was compiled using 140lb (210gsm) card and plenty of masking tape.

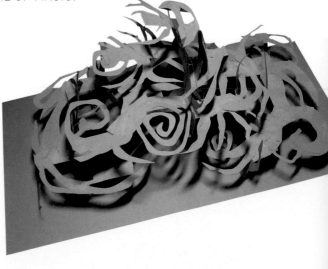

BRIEF HISTORY

Pop-ups were first used in children's books during the latter half of the nineteenth century, though books with parts such as lift-up window flaps were used as far back as the thirteenth century. The high cost of production and an uncertain world economy saw the decline of this expensive book form during the first half of the twentieth century. However, in the late 1950s and 1960s, innovative pop-up books from Czechoslovakia were translated into English, inspiring American designers and publishers to create their own. In turn, their work influenced British designers, and both countries have since produced many remarkable pop-up books and greeting cards.

PAPERS

When practicing the techniques and making roughs, use medium-weight paper. Finished examples, though, should be made with thin, springy card, available from craft supply stores in a range of colors. Squares of this type of card are also used in scrapbooking and cardmaking, and can be bought from craft suppliers in packs.

METHODS

The basic techniques for making incised and multipiece pop-ups are not complex, but when used together they can create designs of remarkable intricacy. As with origami, every new design introduces a technical nuance, and therefore the variations of technique are endless.

Pop-ups must be made very carefully, otherwise they will not collapse flat. Roughs can be made as quickly as necessary, but finished examples need to be made slowly, using a ruler, protractor, and occasionally a template.

Explore the techniques that follow by copying examples from the book and by inventing your own variations. If you have pop-up books or greeting cards on hand, look through them and try to identify the mechanisms that make them work, many of which are explained here.

UNTITLED
PAUL JACKSON
This intricate incised pop-up uses asymmetric pop-up techniques to create a negative/positive diamond form.

INVASIVE SPECIES:
THE LIONFISH!
JEMMA WESTING
This wonderfully detailed multipiece pop-up was designed for a book aimed at informing a young audience about the fish as an invasive species, and goes on to describe the predator's physical features and the environmental context in which it is placed. The reader is supplied with 3-D glasses, to allow them to see how the change in light and color at depth would affect the fish's appearance.

INCISED POP-UPS

A WELL-THOUGHT-OUT, WELL-MADE INCISED POP-UP CAN HAVE AN ELEGANCE UNSURPASSED BY ANY OTHER PAPERCRAFT TECHNIQUE, AND ITS SECRET LIES IN CARE OVER BASIC PRINCIPLES.

SEE ALSO
Creasing and Cutting, pages 12–13
Origami Symbols, pages 16–17

Incised pop-ups are constructed from one sheet of card that has been slit and creased. The card opens to 90 degrees to reveal the pop-up, then, as the card is opened further, the pop-up flattens back into it. Adhesive is seldom used, except perhaps to glue a completed design to a backing sheet for strength.

PRACTICE NOTE
When practicing cutting techniques or working on a design, this one tip will save you a lot of time and paper. If you make a slit in the wrong place, do not discard the sheet to start afresh, instead, seal the slit by taping over it at the back of the sheet, then slit again in the correct position. That way, a slit may be made, taped up, and remade many times.

SINGLE SLIT BASIC EXAMPLE
With the card folded in half, cut in from the crease, then fold the triangles backward and forward along the two creases. Open the card. Pull the triangles upward, recreasing the central fold as a mountain. Fold the card in half and press flat to reinforce the creases.

THE COMPLETED SINGLE-SLIT POP-UP
Note which crease is a mountain: The orientation of the creases is not arbitrary.

SINGLE SLIT VARIATIONS
The single slit in a pop-up can start anywhere along the length of the central crease and can take any shape. The secondary creases can come away from the end of the slit at any angle, as you can see from these examples.

Note the shallow angle of this crease.

Here, the pop-up will pierce the plane of the card.

The crease could run off the bottom edge.

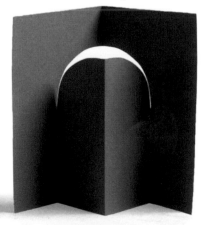

DOUBLE SLIT BASIC EXAMPLE

This technique is very similar to the single slit, but offers greater creative possibilities. As the name suggests, a double slit requires two cuts.

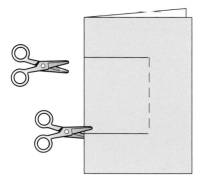

Cut in twice from the central crease, then fold the loose section that lies between the slits backward and forward. Open the card and pull the loose section toward you, recreasing the central fold, on the pop-up strip only, as a mountain. Fold the card in half and press flat to reinforce the creases.

THE COMPLETED DOUBLE-SLIT POP-UP

Note the single mountain crease among four valleys.

DOUBLE SLIT VARIATIONS

As with the single-slit technique, the slits can be of any shape, though the secondary crease must always connect the ends.

A V-shaped double slit. The slits need not be parallel.

This complex variation pierces the plane of the card to create a "front and back" effect.

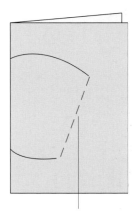

Note that the crease between the ends of the slits is not parallel to the center crease.

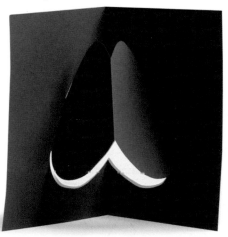

ASYMMETRIC SLITS BASIC EXAMPLE

The previous single- and double-slit examples and variations will all produce symmetrical pop-ups. This is because the card is first folded in half to form a double layer, then cut through both layers to create a slit that is the same shape on both sides of the crease. With careful measurement, however, the symmetry can be broken to make possible a much wider vocabulary of form.

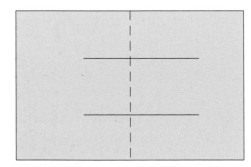

1 Form no creases, but make a measured drawing. Draw the central crease, then draw the two slits that sit asymmetrically across the central crease.

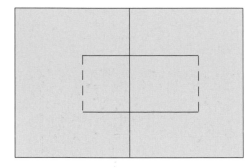

2 Draw two valley creases, parallel to the central crease.

THE COMPLETED ASYMMETRIC POP-UP

This is the result, if all the creases are correctly placed. It is critical to understand which distances are equal—and why—if this useful technique is to be mastered. If you are still unsure of the principles, try remaking this example.

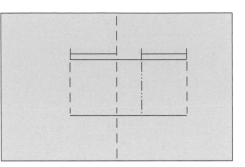

3 Measure the distance from the central crease to the nearer valley crease line. Reproduce that distance to the inside of the other valley crease. This will be the position of the mountain crease.

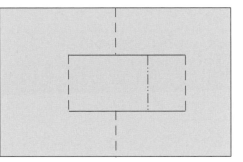

4 Erase that part of the central crease that runs across the pop-up strip. Cut the slits, make the creases (either by hand or by scoring, depending on the weight of the paper or card) and fold to shape.

ASYMMETRIC VARIATIONS

The only rule here is that the two valleys and one mountain that make the pop-up must all be parallel to the central crease. Careful measurement and a clear constructional procedure are key to the successful use of this technique, so before making any creases always draw everything out first, measuring carefully.

NONPARALLEL CREASES

Whatever shapes the techniques shown so far may form, the creases will always be parallel and somewhat boxlike. Here is a way to construct creases that are not parallel but tapered, creating odd perspective effects. A protractor will be needed.

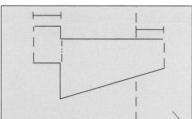

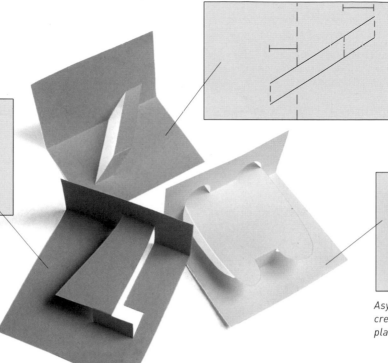

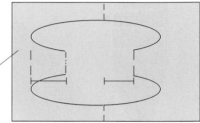

Note the equal distances here and how they are measured horizontally, not at the angle of the band.

Here the shorter plane extends below the longer one, placing the mountain crease between two distinct shapes and not in a seemingly arbitrary position.

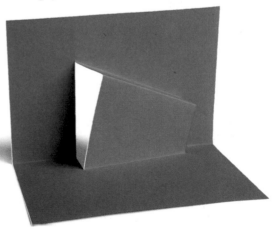

Asymmetric principles are used here to create a form that extends "behind" the plane of the card.

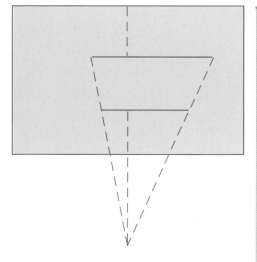

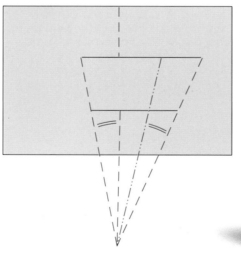

THE COMPLETED NONPARALLEL POP-UP
With this technique it is usually easier and more accurate to form the creases by scoring the paper or card, rather than creasing by hand.

1 The slits are of unequal length, but the creases meet at an imaginary focal point below the card, on the line of the central crease. Draw everything before slitting or creasing

2 To locate the position of the mountain crease, measure the smaller angle between one valley crease and the central crease, then measure the same angle to the inside of the other valley crease. The mountain crease must also radiate from the focal point. When the drawing is complete, slit, crease, and fold to shape.

GENERATIONS BASIC EXAMPLE

Every pop-up is built around an existing crease and generates its own new creases. These new creases can in turn be used to create more pop-ups, which in turn generate new creases that can be used to create more pop-ups, and so on, through successive generations. The principle can be applied to any of the techniques featured so far, or to different techniques at each generation.

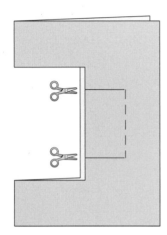

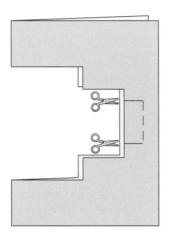

1 Begin with the basic example of the double-slit pop-up, fully formed. Make two cuts into the nearest folded edge and proceed to make a simple double-slit pop-up, identical to the bigger one just made, but smaller.

2 Similarly, now cut into the new nearside folded edge (the one just made), to make another double-slit pop-up. This process can continue through the generations until creases become too small for pop-ups to be formed. Generations can also be cut into central mountain creases to form what might be called "pop-ins," rather than pop-ups.

THE COMPLETED GENERATIONAL POP-UP
Practice this technique whenever you get a spare moment, creating successive generations from single- or double-slit pop-ups.

GENERATIONS VARIATION

A complex form can be built up generation by generation. The form here is symmetrical, but the principle can equally be applied to asymmetric forms that are drawn before being cut. After the third generation is formed the card will not take a doubling of the "steps" with another generation. The large number of creases means that the form takes some force to pull open, but once erected, it will not wilt shut as pop-ups with few creases frequently do.

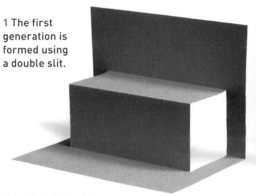

1 The first generation is formed using a double slit.

2 Cutting through all the layers of the first-generation pop-up creates the top and bottom "steps."

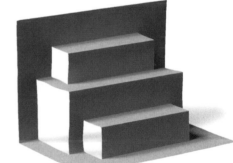

3 The third generation is formed by cutting through all the layers of the second generation.

CUTAWAYS BASIC EXAMPLE

The cutaway technique releases the paper on one side of a crease to create interesting, freestanding forms.

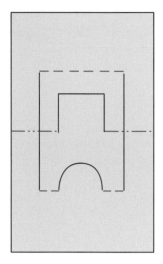

Make the double-slit basic example pop-up. Open it out flat. Incise a semicircular line that begins and ends on the bottom valley crease, and incise three sides of a rectangular shape beginning and ending on the central mountain crease. Re-form the pop-up, but do not crease inside each incision, allowing the semicircular and rectangular forms to stand proud.

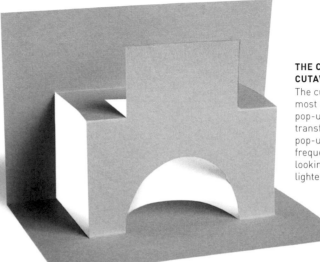

THE COMPLETED CUTAWAY POP-UP

The cutaway is the single most useful of all incised pop-up techniques. It transforms conventional pop-up shapes—which are frequently static and heavy-looking—into forms that are lighter and more dynamic.

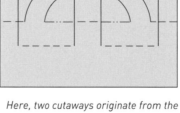

Here, two cutaways originate from the same crease and overlap. The result is a pleasing double cutaway form, projecting forward on each side of the mountain crease.

CUTAWAY VARIATIONS

The application of cutaway techniques is almost infinite, because any shape can be made to project from any crease, as long as the shapes do not collide or leave so little of a crease that the structure becomes very weak. They can be used with any previously described technique or combination of techniques. For finished works, draw the slits and creases onto uncreased card, thereby avoiding creases across the base of all freestanding shapes, then slit and crease. Note the interior spaces created by this technique. They add lightness to a pop-up form and make possible an infinite range of silhouettes.

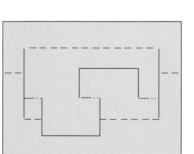

The cutaway arch bridges the gap between two conventional double-slit pop-ups, leaving an interesting negative shape.

MULTIPIECE POP-UPS

MULTIPIECE POP-UPS ARE MADE FROM MANY PIECES OF SHAPED CARD, STUCK TO A BACKING SHEET THAT OPENS AND CLOSES TO REVEAL OR ENCLOSE THE POP-UP. WHEREAS WITH INCISED POP-UPS THE BACKING SHEET OPENS TO 90 DEGREES FOR EFFECT, WITH MULTIPIECE DESIGNS IT OPENS FLAT, TO 180 DEGREES.

This technique requires more construction than the incising methods, but creates forms that are more sculptural.

MATERIALS

Roughs can be made from medium- or heavyweight paper, but finished works should be constructed from thin, springy card. The backing sheet may need to be a heavy card, or even board, depending on the stresses imposed by the pop-up. Remember to use strong glue for the finished construction, applying it sparingly to the tabs.

SEE ALSO

Creasing and Cutting, pages 12–13
Origami Symbols, pages 16–17

HORIZONTAL V BASIC EXAMPLE

This is the simplest 180-degree pop-up technique.

1 Cut out a rectangle of medium- or heavyweight paper. Crease it down the center, then crease it across the bottom. Make a short slit at the bottom edge to separate two tabs.

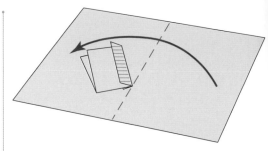

2 Fold the paper rectangle in half, so that the tabs are on the outside. Apply glue to each tab. Make a valley crease down the center of the backing sheet. Stick one tab to the backing sheet, so that the central crease on the backing sheet touches the crease on the pop-up. Fold the other half of the backing sheet on top, so that it sticks to the other tab.

THE COMPLETED HORIZONTAL V

Opening out the backing sheet reveals the pop-up. The key here is to make the crease on the backing sheet lie exactly beneath the crease on the pop-up.

HORIZONTAL V VARIATIONS

Almost every element of the horizontal V is variable, as long as the pop-up crosses the crease on the backing sheet. For example: the crease on the pop-up can move to one side of the paper; the pop-up piece can be of any size; the V-shaped angle across the crease on the backing sheet can be anything between 1 and about 175 degrees (but not completely straight); the crease across the bottom of the pop-up shape need not be at 90 degrees to the vertical crease; and the angles of the V on each side of the crease on the backing sheet need not be the same. The letter B, the arch, and the house examples here illustrate the variety of forms made possible by changing the angle between the arms of the V piece.

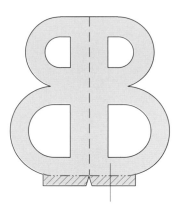

The arms of the V, in this case mirror images of a letter B, are folded back against each other, so that the V is shut tight. The tabs run along the crease on the backing sheet.

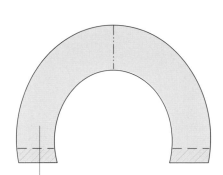

The angle of the crease in the center of the arch is almost perpendicular to the central crease on the backing sheet.

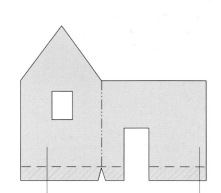

The house shape is made by altering the silhouette of the "wall" seen opposite.

UPTURNED V BASIC EXAMPLE

This method is similar to the horizontal V technique, except that now the V goes up and over the crease on the backing sheet, not flat across it.

1 Cut out a rectangle of paper. Make a mountain crease across the middle and two valleys across the ends.

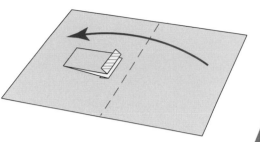

2 Fold the paper in half, along the mountain. Fold back the tabs and apply glue to each one. Make a valley crease down the center of the backing sheet. Glue one tab to the backing sheet, parallel to, but a little way away from, its central crease. Fold the other half of the sheet on top, to stick to the other tab.

THE COMPLETED UPTURNED V

Opening out the backing sheet reveals the pop-up. Using this method is an effective way to achieve height in a pop-up.

UPTURNED V VARIATIONS

As with the horizontal V, almost every element of the upturned V is variable. For example: the paper rectangle can be of any size; the V can become an X; the V can be placed asymmetrically on the backing sheet; and the tab creases need not be parallel to the crease on the backing sheet.

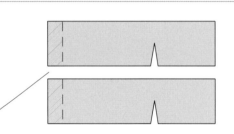

Two pieces interlocked at the slits create an X-shaped pop-up. The form can, of course, be made considerably more complex than this example.

Here, the angle of the tabs tapers. If the creases were extended, they would meet exactly at the central crease. For this reason, the pop-up has to be placed precisely on the backing sheet.

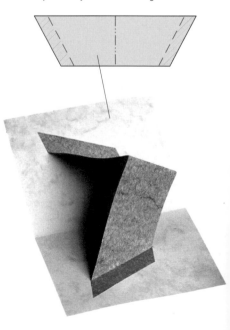

The mountain crease need not be placed in the center of the pop-up, but can be placed to one side.

LAYERING BASIC EXAMPLE

This technique provides a series of raised horizontal planes, like the tiers of a wedding cake.

THE COMPLETED LAYER POP-UP

The pop-up will fold in half and collapse flat when the backing sheet is folded inward.

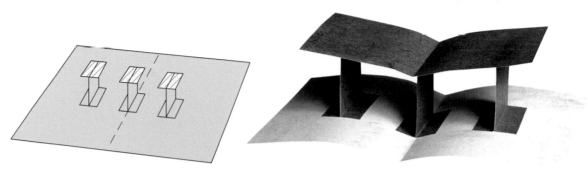

1 Construct three identical pillars, creased as above. Apply glue to the entire surface, then fold in half.

2 Crease the center of a sheet of stiff card. Glue the pillars to a backing sheet of stiff card, one along the crease on the card and one on each side, parallel to the crease. Cut out a rectangle of paper and glue it to the tops of the pillars. The paper must have a crease directly over the central pillar.

LAYERING VARIATIONS

Layering is the most sculptural of all pop-up techniques, and the most illusory (the layers appear to be unsupported). The rule here is that there must be at least three supporting pillars, one along the crease on the backing sheet and one to each side, parallel to that crease. However, other aspects of a layered pop-up are variable. For example: the top layer can be of any shape; the pillars need not be symmetrically distributed; and the pop-up can be used as the base for more layers on top, or as a base for other 180-degree pop-up techniques.

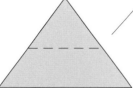

With complex constructions the key is to work layer by layer, making sure that each layer can be folded flat before moving up to the next.

The asymmetry of this shape means that a wider pillar needs to be built under the wider side of the shape.

Four pillars are needed for this design, two along the central crease and one on each side.

BOXES

POP-UP BOXES USE MULTIPIECE TECHNIQUES TO CONSTRUCT ENCLOSED FORMS. THEY CAN BE PLACED ON ANY CREASE THAT OPENS 180 DEGREES. THE SIDES MAKE A 90-DEGREE ANGLE WITH THE BACKING SHEET, WHICH CAN BE THE SUPPORT FOR ANY 90-DEGREE OR INCISED TECHNIQUES.

No division relies on guesswork or trial and error: each is made by folding one specific point to another, and each can be proved accurate using geometric or trigonometric theorems. They are all quick and reliable, and do not require the use of a protractor, ruler, or pencil. More important, they are all supremely elegant. Surprisingly, there is not just one way to divide an edge or fold a polygon, but many. Some methods are direct, while others are more complex, revealing unexpected and satisfying edge or crease alignments during the construction.

SEE ALSO
....
Creasing and Cutting, pages 12–13
Origami Symbols, pages 16–17

SQUARE-ON BOX
The term "square on" refers to the position of the box over the crease of the backing card.

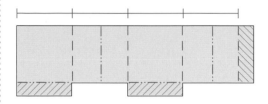

Cut out the above shape, creating tabs where shown. Glue the end tab to the opposite end of the strip to create a square tube. Glue the lower tabs to the creased backing sheet, aligning the central valley fold of the box template with the crease on the backing sheet.

THE COMPLETED SQUARE-ON BOX
When the box is pulled open to stand square, its two mid-face creases should be directly above the crease on the backing sheet.

SQUARE-ON BOX VARIATIONS
The square-on box may be elongated to become wider, deeper, or higher. Some of the creases can be added or removed to create other shapes, such as hexagons and cylinders. Structures with an odd number of sides, such as triangles and pentagons, are more complex to construct, but are a good technical exercise for the novice paper engineer.

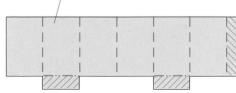

A hexagonal box will require more creases than a square.

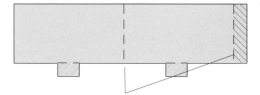

The two creases for a cylinder shape should be positioned on the crease of the backing sheet.

DIAGONAL BOX

Again, the term "diagonal" refers to the box's position in relation to the crease of the backing card.

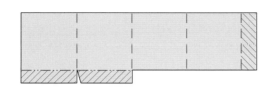

1 Cut out the above shape. Glue the end tab to the opposite end of the strip to create a square tube.

2 Glue the lower tabs to a backing sheet, one on each side of the central crease, so that the crease on the backing sheet lies exactly beneath the diagonal of the box. To make a box with 90-degree corners, glue the tabs at 45 degrees to the central crease.

THE COMPLETED DIAGONAL BOX

The diagonal box is perhaps a more elegant structure than previous boxes, because it holds its shape better. Nonsquare boxes can be made if the tabs are not glued at 45 degrees to the central crease.

MAKING A LID

A diagonal box can be topped off with a two-part lid.

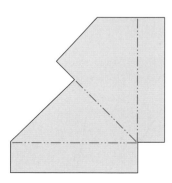

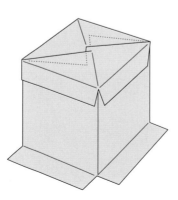

1 To create a lid, make two identical lid sections as shown. Note the creases and tabs.

2 Glue one lid piece to the two faces of the box already tabbed to the backing sheet, and the other to the other two faces.

THE COMPLETED LID

The two lid halves will interlock when the backing sheet is opened and the box formed.

PROJECT

POP-UP SPIDER

THIS VIBRANT, COLORFUL PROJECT ILLUSTRATES HOW YOU CAN BUILD UPON THE BASIC PRINCIPLES OF THE V FOLD TO CREATE EXCITING AND REALISTIC MULTIPIECE POP-UP DESIGNS. FOR EASE OF WORKING, AND TO ENSURE THE SURFACES OF THE CARD REMAIN CLEAN, ALWAYS ALLOW THE GLUE TO DRY BEFORE CONTINUING TO EACH NEW STAGE.

WHAT YOU WILL NEED

- 3 sheets of 140lb (210gsm) letter size (A4) card, of different colors, here bright orange, red, and yellow
- 1 sheet of 160lb (240gsm) letter size (A4) card, white: if you have difficulty finding 160lb (240gsm), use any card that is thicker than the card used for the pop-up pieces, but that will fold in the middle
- Pencil
- Craft knife
- Cutting mat
- Metal ruler
- PVA glue, to keep the work clean you may find it easier to use a tube of glue with a dispensing nozzle
- Fine paintbrush (optional), to apply the glue if not using a tube
- Protractor

SEE ALSO

Creasing and Cutting, pages 12–13
Multipiece Pop-ups, pages 52–55

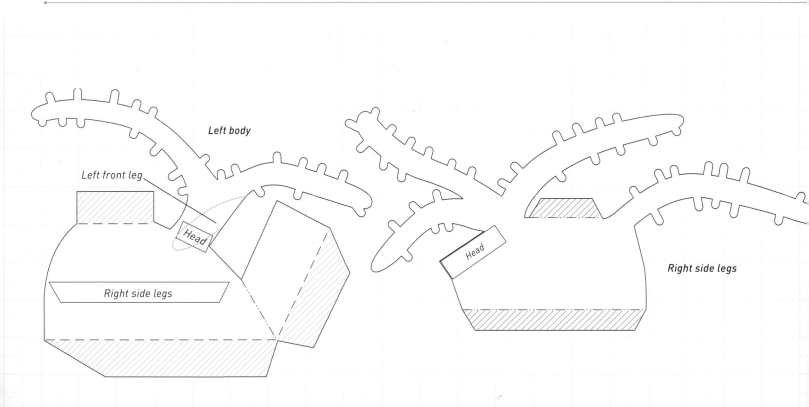

Left body

Left front leg

Head

Right side legs

Head

Right side legs

TEMPLATES

The templates are illustrated slighly smaller. To reproduce the spider exactly, photocopy the templates at 125%, cut them out, and draw around them onto your colored card.

TIPS

When creating a fold line, score the line from the other side of the template—it'll fold much easier!

If you're not happy using a knife to score, try using a scoring stylus or a ballpoint pen that has run out of ink. The aim is to compress the fibers of the card so that it can fold and flex but not break.

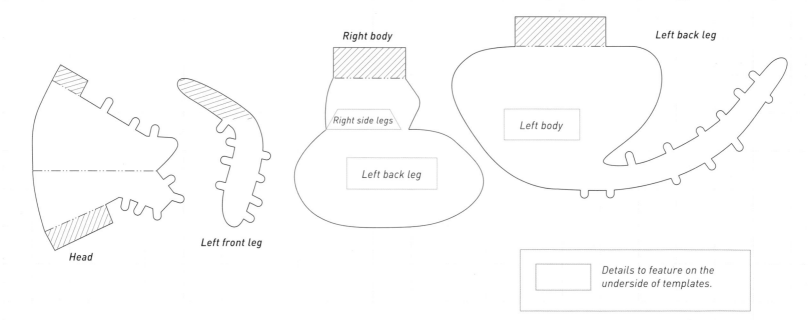

Right body

Right side legs

Left back leg

Left body

Left back leg

Left front leg

Head

Left back leg

Left body

Details to feature on the underside of templates.

1 Use a pencil to transfer the spider templates to the colored card. Using a craft knife with a sharp blade, and working on a cutting mat, carefully cut out all of the pieces.

4 Apply PVA glue thinly where indicated on the template to the left front leg. Hold the left body piece with the tabs facing toward you and fix the left front leg to the back of and below the two legs.

6 Apply glue to the right tab of the head and position it on the right side legs. Allow the glue to dry.

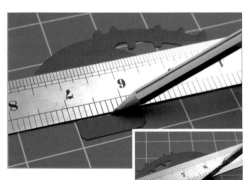

2 Use the craft knife and a metal ruler to score all the fold lines. Refer to the templates to ascertain which should be mountain creases and which are valleys.

3 Make the folds and use a pencil to mark the places where the various elements will be adhered, as indicated on the templates.

5 Apply glue to the longer tab of the right side legs piece, and fix this in position on the left body.

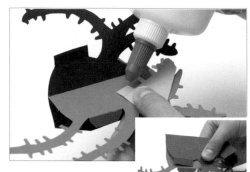

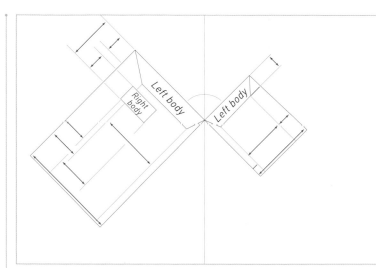

Drawing plan for Step 9

7 Once the right tab is dry, apply glue to the remaining tab on the head. Fold the left body piece down onto the glued tab on the head to finish fixing this section.

8 Apply glue to the overhanging tab of the right side legs piece and attach to the right body where indicated on the template.

9 Using the drawing plan above right as a guide, fold the sheet of 160lb (240gsm) card in half. Measure 4in. (10cm) along the crease from the top and mark the positions for the fixing tabs of the left body pieces, at 45 degrees to the crease. You can draw the shapes of the remaining tabs on the left body onto the base card—do this by simply lining up the longest sides of the tabs against the 45-degree angle mark. You can then draw around your tab to get the exact shape. The longer and closer side of the left body sits 1¼in. (3cm) away from the furthest side of the right body and is directly parallel to it. Draw the right body tab mark by going in toward the spine by ⅝in. (1.5cm) and use the remaining tab on the bottom of the right body piece to draw around to get your positioned spot.

10 Apply glue to the remaining tabs on the left and right body, then fix the structure you have so far to the base, taking care to ensure that it is lined up correctly.

11 Apply glue to the exposed tab on the left back leg piece and the tab on the left body, then fix the left back leg to the left body and the right body, taking care with alignment. Once in place, carefully close the card flat and leave to dry.

POP-UP SPIDER
Give the completed spider pop-up to a friend to open for a great surprise.

COLORED PAPERS

Using colored papers for sculpting can make a cheerful departure from the more traditional white.

UNIT 3

PAPER SCULPTURE

SCULPTING IN PAPER IS JUST AS CREATIVE AS WORKING IN WOOD, METAL, OR STONE, AND LIKE ALL TRUE ART, IT CAN BE PRACTICED AND ENJOYED AT ANY LEVEL. EVEN THE INEXPERIENCED CAN PRODUCE ATTRACTIVE SCULPTURES THAT WILL GIVE PLEASURE TO THEMSELVES AND OTHERS.

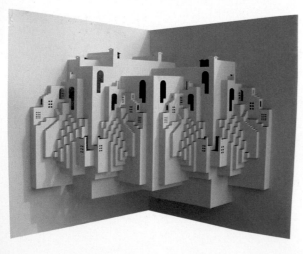

ABSTRACT
INGRID SILIAKUS

Fabricating and designing intriguing sculptures takes time, and for some is a meditative process. For Siliakus the biggest attraction is the end result, which almost always looks more attractive than she had imagined.

PRESERVE
JEFFREY NISHINAKA

Jeffrey Nishinaka's relief paper sculptures make use of slightly raised pieces that are scored and curved to create different angles and gradations of light. You can see the scores at the bottom of the clouds, on the bird's feathers, and in the horizontal ripple at the base of the mountains. Scoring the paper creates crisp, clean folds whereas curving helps to create the three-dimensional illusion seen in the trunks of the trees.

At the same time, paper sculpture has practical applications, too. It is widely used in the teaching of art and design, for education generally, and in displays, exhibitions, advertising, and book illustration.

Broadly speaking, paper sculptures fall under one of two categories. Full-round sculptures can be viewed from all sides, while half-round or low-relief sculptures are designed to be viewed from the front only. The effect of light and shade is an important factor in the completed sculpture, and the artist will need to consider how best to exploit this when working out the original design and selecting the arrangement of the basic forms.

PAPERS

Paper sculpture is traditionally carried out using white paper, which is readily available in various weights. The best choice for the beginner is cartridge paper. Particularly large structures can be made from heavier paper, but this is more difficult to work. At the other extreme, ordinary printer or photocopy paper is quite suitable for small, low-relief subjects.

Colored cartridge paper, available in a wide range of shades, makes an attractive departure from tradition. Remember, though, that colored paper often has a sheen on one side only, and you will get the best effect when light falls on the sculpture if you use the matte surface as the face side. Also, be sure to choose papers that have the color right through; papers that are colored on the surface only will show a white line when cut or scored.

Gold, silver, and other metallic foil papers are frequently used to enhance a sculpture, but they have little or no inherent strength and need to be glued to a sheet of cartridge paper before use. They also have no depth to their decorative surface so cannot be scored.

Giftwrap offers a host of designs that can be used to great effect. The paper can be backed, like foil, or designs cut out and applied to sections of a sculpture.

Mounting board, thin card (in a variety of thicknesses), and corrugated cardboard can be used to make armatures and display bases. Modern styrofoam sheets can be especially useful, combining lightness with rigidity.

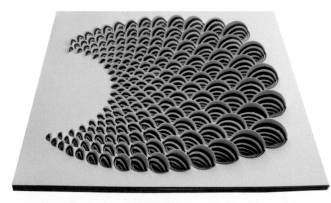

PAPER SCALES, MATTHEW SHLIAN
As a paper engineer, Matthew Shlian's work is rooted in print media, book arts, and commercial design. Beginning with an initial fold, a single action causes a transfer of energy to subsequent folds, which ultimately manifest in drawings and three-dimensional forms. Shlian states that his focus is on the process rather than the final product.

WARPED STELLATION MATTHEW SHLIAN
Matthew Shlian uses his paper-engineering skills to create kinetic sculptures that have led to collaborations with scientists at the University of Michigan, working on the nanoscale and translating paper structures to micro-origami. Researchers see paper engineering as a metaphor for scientific principles, whereas Shlian sees their inquiries as a basis for artistic inspiration.

CONES AND CYLINDERS

THE ESSENCE OF PAPER SCULPTURE IS REPRESENTATIONAL SHAPE. THE SHALLOW FORM OF A LEAF, OR A FACIAL MASK PRODUCED PERHAPS BY SCORING AND FOLDING, RELIES ON THE BASIC STRUCTURAL FORMS OF CONE AND CYLINDER, SHAPES THAT CAN BE PRODUCED USING THE BENDING, SCORING, AND FOLDING TECHNIQUES DETAILED ON PAGES 12–13.

MULTIPLE USES

A cone may be used in a variety of ways, for example as the body of a full-round sculpture or, in a very shallow form, the eye of a low-relief figure. Cylinders of different sizes may be used as the body and neck of a full-round figure, as internal spacers in a construction, or as a supporting or decorative column in a design. The simple cylinder is not very strong, but may be transformed into a load-bearing structure by scoring and bending.

SEE ALSO
Creasing and Cutting, pages 12–13
Origami Symbols, pages 16–17

BASIC CONES

Circular cones may be used to represent many things in paper sculpture, and their natural rigidity makes them an ideal base on which to build.

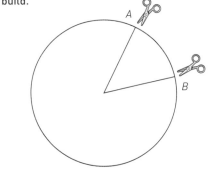

Cut a triangular segment from a circular piece of paper, as shown. Apply glue fully along edge A and make up the cone by overlapping edge B onto A.

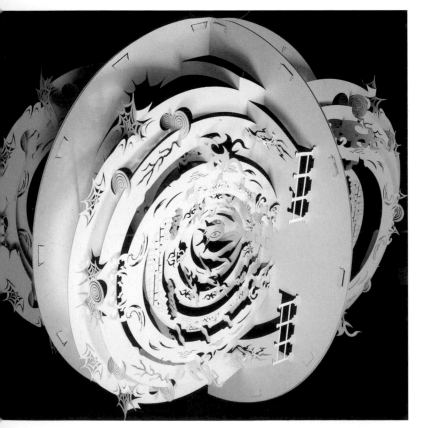

INNERRINGS
INGRID SILIAKUS

This sculpture is designed using four outer white sides and two inner black ones, all cut and folded out of a separate piece of card. The outer rings are positioned in different dimensions, within which are cut and folded motifs symbolic of the basic elements, such as water and fire, along with figures and other shapes with symbolic value.

Two of the opposite parts in the outer section are invisibly attached to each other by means of pins and slots on the edges. These locks can be opened, after which the object can be folded inward into a two-dimensional shape.

CONE SELECTION

Varying either the radius of the circle or the size of the segment that is cut away produces cones of different diameters and heights. The latter will give cones of differing diameter and height from a circle of the same size.

CONCENTRIC SCORED CONES

Variations in this cone are made by adjusting the distance between the scored lines, which must always alternate between valley and mountain crease.

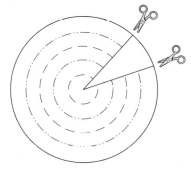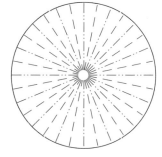

Cut out a circle of paper and score concentric circles alternately on the face and reverse side of the paper. In this instance each circle increases in radius by 1in. (25mm) to give an overall diameter of 10in. (250mm). Cut away a triangular segment of the circle and complete as for the basic cone.

PLEATED CONES

Variations in this cone are made by adjusting the distance between the scored lines, which must always alternate between valley and mountain crease.

Make alternate face and reverse scores that radiate out from the center of the paper circle, with the help of accurate measurement and careful folding, to give a pleated effect. Gluing will be easier if a small circle is removed from the center of the cone.

BASIC CYLINDERS

Basic cylinders are simply formed by rolling a rectangular piece of paper. Leaving a tab or overlap when cutting to the required size will make it easy to form the completed cylinder.

SCORED CYLINDERS

A rectangular piece of paper scored, as shown, on the concave side will produce a cylinder with a recessed curved surface. The paper is fastened together against the natural curve, and between the scores the curve is manipulated over a wooden dowel to achieve the fluted effect.

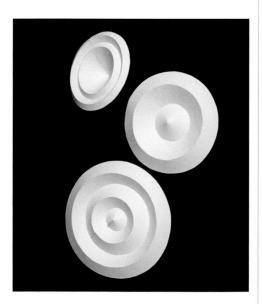

SCORED CONE SELECTION
You can clearly see the difference in distance between scored lines on these cones. As with the basic cone, the size of the cutaway segment will determine the height and diameter of the completed cone: the largest cone here was produced by removing a 30-degree segment.

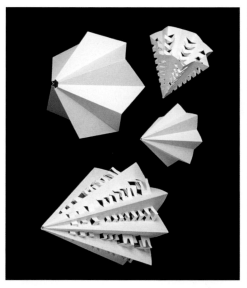

PLEATED CONE SELECTION
Different sizes of starting circle will produce cones of varying height and diameters. The surface pattern is achieved by cutting across the reverse scores.

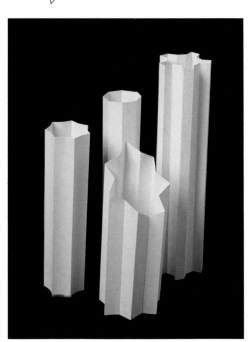

DECORATIVE FORMS

COMBINATIONS OF STRAIGHT AND CURVED SCORES CAN PRODUCE A MULTITUDE OF INTERESTING AND DECORATIVE FORMS, IDEAL FOR PANEL AND BORDER DECORATION AND DISPLAY WORK.

SEE ALSO

Creasing and Cutting, pages 12–13
Origami Symbols, pages 16–17

COMPOUND SURFACE SCORING

Surface design can be achieved by compound scoring, always on the face side. The simple surface design on the larger example is the result of straight scoring with the paper curved for effect; dimensions are a matter of choice, but the marking out needs to be accurate. The same design has also been developed into a cylindrical shape, together with a cylinder using curved scores for its surface design.

STRAIGHT SCORING

Accurate scoring is the key to achieving the desired effect.

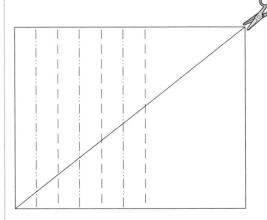

Score a rectangular piece of paper alternately on face and reverse sides at ½in. (1.3cm) intervals, as shown. Cut the paper diagonally, then, working on a flat surface, apply glue to the base of each pleat at one end only. Pinch the pleats together.

STRAIGHT-SCORED SHAPE

The two shapes obtained from a single piece of paper may be used to produce the leaf effect.

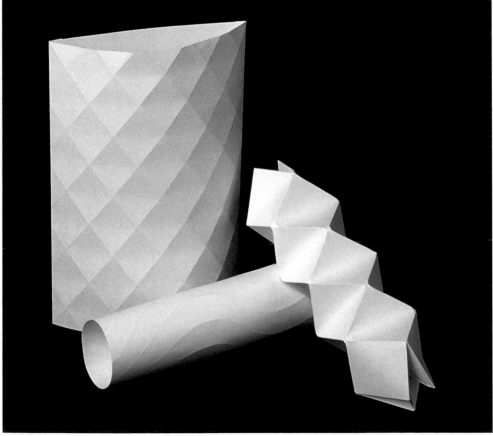

CURVED SCORING

Many designs are produced by the use of curved scoring, and a combination of carefully placed mountain and valley creases can create flowing relief forms.

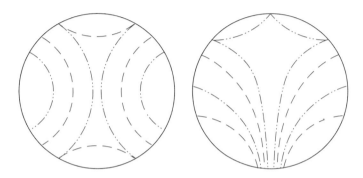

When planning a design, draw the creases onto the paper shape first, either freehand or using a drawing compass. Score and bend each crease into shape, using controlled pressure and taking your time—if you are too forceful the paper will buckle.

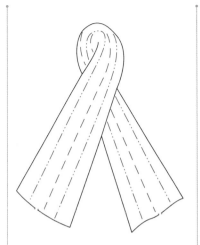

One arm of a U-shape scored with alternate mountain and valley creases, as shown, can be bent across the other.

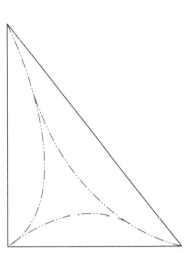

Three mountain scores in a triangle create this cushion-like form.

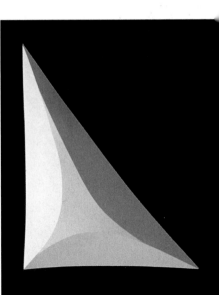

CURVED SCORING SELECTION

The technique of curved scoring produces forms with movement and expression, as you can see in the examples here and over the page.

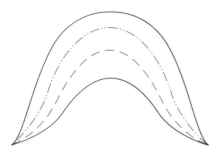

This example is similar to the two crossed-over shapes below, but more open.

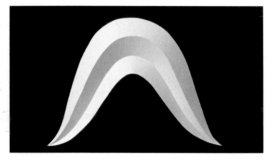

Only the mountain crease reaches to the end of the tail of this shape. Apply glue where the two tails cross over each other to hold the curl in position.

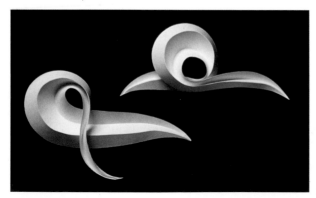

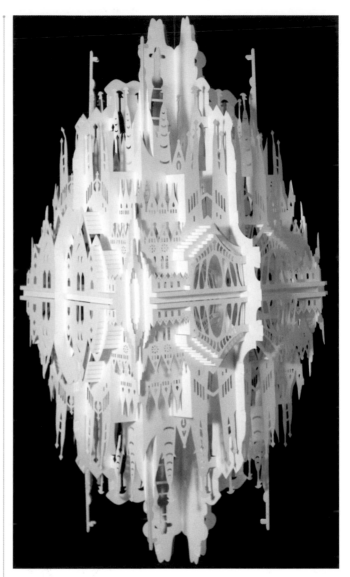

REFLECTION ON SAGRADA FAMILIA
INGRID SILIAKUS

When planning her remarkably detailed architecture sculptures, Ingrid Siliakus undertakes much research, gathering photographs, architectural maps, and plans. When all the information is in, it is studied and decisions made regarding which side of the building is the most suitable to translate into a piece of paper architecture.

The design starts with a drawing that details valley and mountain folds and necessary cuts. The drawing is cut and folded to see the result, then adjustments and additions are made to the design. Again, the drawing is cut and folded, a process that can result in up to 30 prototypes.

LIGHTING

A relief sculpture owes its impact almost exclusively to the way it is lit. Light is less vital to a three-dimensional, freestanding sculpture, however it still has the power to make a good piece look superb. Experienced sculptors try to consider the effects of light from the moment they begin a design.

Always light a relief sculpture from a single source at the side or above. Front lighting does not create shadows and makes the relief appear flat and uninteresting, while side lighting produces a play of light and shade across the surface. With these considerations in mind, decide carefully where to best place your sculpture for optimum effect.

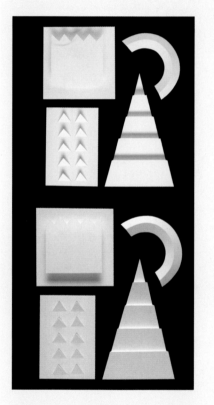

EFFECTIVE AND INEFFECTIVE LIGHTING

Compare and contrast the play of light and shadow over the surface of the shapes in these two examples, the first lit from the bottom and the second lit from the top. Depending on how the light hits the folds of the shapes, in some cases cast shadows create the impression of depth, whereas some of the folds do not cast shadows and so get lost.

TEXTURED SURFACES

A range of expressive textures can be created by scoring and cutting the surface of the paper.

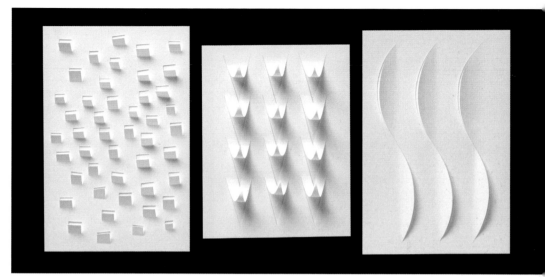

Cut texturing will only be visible if it creates a pattern of light and shadow, so think about where the piece will be lit from before cutting.

GOLDEN GATE BRIDGE
JEFFREY NISHINAKA

When Jeffrey Nishinaka photographs his relief paper sculptures, he ensures that his light source is at an angle that is more or less level with the piece, almost pointing away and barely skimming the surface of the sculpture. This creates a more dramatic lighting effect and brings out the illusion of three-dimensionality. In addition here, the clouds are lit from behind, using small, regular incandescent bulbs, similar to Christmas tree lights. The clouds are cut away from the background to fit the bulbs in position.

ASSEMBLY AND ARMATURES

WHEN IT COMES TO COMBINING THE VARIOUS PAPER SHAPES TO CREATE THE COMPLETE SCULPTURE, THERE ARE A NUMBER OF ASSEMBLY METHODS TO CHOOSE FROM. FOR SOME DESIGNS YOU CAN USE ADHESIVES ALONE, WHILE FOR OTHERS YOU WILL FIND TABS INVALUABLE. SOME SCULPTURES WILL NECESSITATE THE USE OF AN ARMATURE, AN UNSEEN INTERNAL SUPPORTING STRUCTURE.

ASSEMBLY

When assembling your sculpture, sometimes adhesive tape, double-sided tape, or an unseen staple may be all that is needed. However, for most fastenings, use a good-quality glue that is quick drying but that allows you time to change your mind. Adhesive pads are useful when mounting a half-round or low-relief sculpture for display, and you can easily remove the sculpture by slicing through the pad.

Alternatively, you can use tabs to attach one component to another, or a half-round sculpture to its armature. These can be separate or integral.

ARMATURES

A full-round sculpture needs an internal support that generally follows the shape of the sculpture and enables other components to be built onto it. A medium-sized full-round sculpture may have as its central support a rolled paper cylinder, a poster tube, or a wooden dowel, with suitable crosspieces if necessary.

A half-round or low-relief sculpture is built up in layers and usually requires a flat armature that both supports the components and keeps the sculpture in shape. The armature has the same profile as the sculpture, but on a slightly smaller scale, so that the sculpture can be attached to it by means of tabs.

SEE ALSO

Cones and cylinders, pages 64–65
Decorative forms, pages 66–69

TABBING METHODS

Tabs can either be an integral part of the shape being cut, or be made from strips of paper attached to the shape. Separate tabs are attached to the inside of the component part of the sculpture, giving it a smooth unbroken contour, so are generally preferable to integral tabs when the contours are visible.

1 Cut integral tabs as part of the component. Mark and make slits the same width as the tabs in the places where the tabs will meet the armature or backing sheet.

2 Alternatively, cut suitable strips of paper to make separate tabs. Attach these tabs to the underside and just inside the component using glue or adhesive tape. Make slits the same width as the tabs in the places where they will meet the armature or backing sheet.

3 Pull each tab through its corresponding slit until a tight fit is achieved. Bend each tab over and secure in place with adhesive tape or glue.

HALF-ROUND AND LOW-RELIEF ARMATURES

For many half-round sculptures, the armature itself is built up in sections with suitable spacers, such as rolled paper coils, giving the effect of depth to the completed work. For small sculptures, card is often adequate, but for large structures the armature may be made of masonite, plywood, or styrofoam board. Do not overlook the possibilities of readily obtainable corrugated cardboard. This has little rigidity, but makes a perfectly good armature if two layers are glued together with the corrugations at right angles. Be careful, however, if you opt for an armature of flat card. This is liable to warp, and it is wise to cover both sides of the card with cartridge paper.

2 Affix the paper elements to the armature pieces using tabs or adhesive methods. The lower leg in this example is reversed to illustrate how paper is fitted to the armature piece using tabs. Adding paper to the armature is a layering process that builds height and depth.

1 Use a craft knife to cut the basic shape of the armature, onto which the paper elements of the sculpture will be added. This armature features three seperate elements. Details such as fur and facial features are not included on the armature.

3 When all the paper elements have been added, fix any separate pieces onto the main sculpture. In this example the rear front and hind legs are spaced away from the back of the main body using rolled paper coils.

NIGHTFLIGHT

THIS LOW-RELIEF SCULPTURE OF
AN OWL IN FLIGHT SHOWS HOW
THE TECHNIQUES DESCRIBED IN
THE PRECEDING PAGES BUILD
INTO A FINISHED DESIGN.

The owl has a wingspan of 16in. (40cm) and
a height of 17in. (42cm). When completed,
it should be spaced slightly away from the
surface of a display board to give a three-
dimensional effect.

   The armature pieces should be made using
thin card, whereas all the sculpture pieces
can be made using cartridge paper. Feather
effects are cut and raised, and edges are
fringed to the approximate depth indicated
on the templates.

WHAT YOU WILL NEED
....
• Thin card
• Cartridge paper
• Craft knife
• Cutting mat
• Scissors
• PVA glue
• Paintbrush

NIGHTFLIGHT
Careful layering, shaping, and scoring can
create a convincing illusion of depth and
volume, even though the sculpture is in
very low relief.

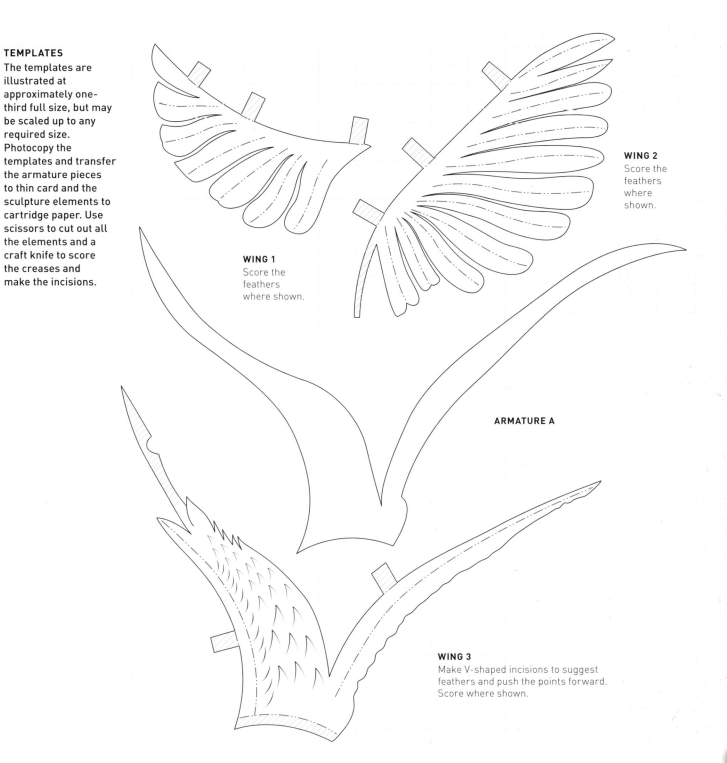

TEMPLATES

The templates are illustrated at approximately one-third full size, but may be scaled up to any required size. Photocopy the templates and transfer the armature pieces to thin card and the sculpture elements to cartridge paper. Use scissors to cut out all the elements and a craft knife to score the creases and make the incisions.

WING 1
Score the feathers where shown.

WING 2
Score the feathers where shown.

ARMATURE A

WING 3
Make V-shaped incisions to suggest feathers and push the points forward. Score where shown.

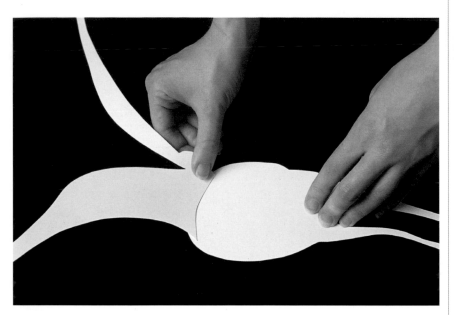

1 Apply glue to the marked area at the top of armature B, and fix armature A in place.

2 Position wing pieces 1 and 2 over the wing armature and glue the narrow strip at the bottom of wing 2 to the armature. Position body piece 1 over the body armature. The unit is wider than the armature, so curve it forward to make it narrower. Fold the tabs on the body and wing pieces to the back of the armature pieces and glue in place.

3 Attach wing piece 3 over the top of wing pieces 1 and 2, using the tabs. Glue the tip of wing 3 to wing 2. Glue the base of wing 3 to the base of the wing armature. Position body piece 2 to body 1, slightly higher on the left than on the right, to accentuate the illusion of a solid body thrusting forward. Fold the tabs over and fix them to the back of the armature.

4 Position eye pieces 1 and 2 next to each other, with the central fringe overlapping and bending up, and glue the beak in position. Glue eye sections 3 and 4 in position over 1 and 2. Attach separate tabs to the back of each pupil and use them to attach the face to body piece 2.

5 To finish, use glue to attach the tail and feather pieces to the back of armature B.

ARMATURE B

BODY 1

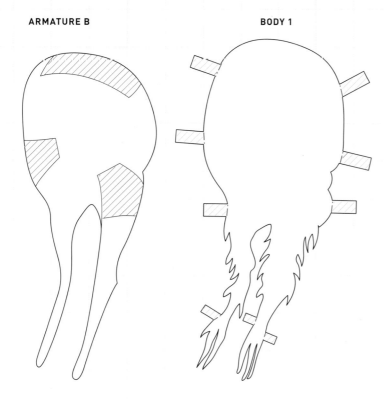

EYE 1 AND 2
Mirror images of each other. For each, cut out the center. Cut to center from the outer edge and glue A over B to form a shallow cone. Score around the perimeter, then cut the fringe.

EYE 3 AND 4
For each, cut from the edge to the center and score where shown. Overlap the cut edge to form a shallow cone and glue. When dry, trim off the edge to leave a very narrow flange.

BODY 2
Make V-shaped incisions to suggest feathers and push the points forward. Make a mountain score to allow the right-hand section to curve upward.

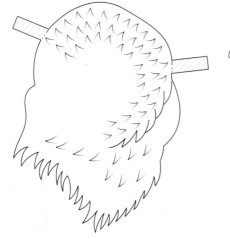

FEATHER
Curl the feathers over a scissor blade.

TAIL

BEAK

BOOKBINDING AWL
A heavy-duty awl is used to punch holes in several sheets of paper.

UNIT 4

BOOK-BINDING

BOOKBINDING ALLOWS YOU TO CREATE SOMETHING THAT IS BOTH BEAUTIFUL AND FUNCTIONAL, WHILE ALSO INDULGING A LOVE OF PAPER. PAPER IS, OF COURSE, AN ESSENTIAL COMPONENT OF BOOKBINDING, AND THERE IS DELIGHT TO BE HAD IN SELECTING PAPERS OF SPECIFIC COLORS, WEIGHTS, AND TEXTURES TO SUIT A PARTICULAR BOOKBINDING PROJECT.

PASTE BRUSHES
Round-headed brushes are the most suitable for applying paste. You will need at least one, but ideally a selection of three in different sizes.

OUT FOR A WALK
HANNAH BROWN
Bookbinding techniques allow you to personalize your own note- or address books, or even add covers to existing written pages. Hannah Brown has taken an existing lined and sewn notebook, divided up and lettered the pages to turn it into an address book, and sewn on a card cover decorated with found objects.

HEADLAMP
HANNAH BROWN
This case binding, made up of six sections sewn together on three tapes, features a book cloth cover and attachments including ribbons, a safety pin, and jewelry chain link.

PAPERS

A book's pages need to be able to withstand repeated opening and handling, so consider usings card-weight paper. Watercolor paper, printmaking paper, and calligraphy papers work well, as do stiffer handmade papers. These papers can also be used to make soft covers. Ordinary photocopy paper can take some wear and tear, so you can choose to use this for the pages of a notebook. Photo albums and scrapbooks, however, require sturdier pages.

Hard covers are made from boards covered with paper or book cloth. Regular cardboard is too thin and vulnerable to piercing to use for bookbinding, so millboard or pasteboard are used instead. Millboard is the strongest and highest quality board. However, it is very dense and difficult to cut by hand. Pasteboard is of medium density and so easier to cut and less expensive to buy, and is available from good art supply stores.

A pliable and sturdy cover material is usually glued to a board. Look for paper that is thin enough to fold neatly around the corners and produce tight, crisp points and edges. Very thick paper will not fold neatly and is difficult to make into a point. Book cloth is another option. This is a cotton-based material with a paper backing that ensures that the adhesive does not penetrate the cloth.

ADHESIVES

Adhesives are referred to as either pastes or glues. Paste is made from wheat flour cooked with water to create an inexpensive, effective adhesive. Its slow-drying characteristic makes it very useful when positioning and repositioning a board on cover paper. It is applied with a brush and must be refrigerated to prevent spoiling. PVA glue is quick drying and an excellent complement to wheat paste: store it in a small cone-topped bottle for handy application and airtight storage.

BINDING MATERIALS

There are many options when selecting a binding material, such as colorful embroidery threads, linen bookbinding threads, ribbon, and raffia. Select a material that best suits the overall look and functionality of the book. For a sewn multisection book, a thin, strong bookbinding thread will secure the sections tightly.

Coating binding thread with a thin layer of beeswax helps the thread to pass through the holes smoothly and makes it grip the paper once in place. Decorative ribbons should not be waxed; embroidery and bookbinding threads should. Alternatively, look for waxed linen thread in the beading section of your local craft store.

BINDING THREADS
Remember when choosing a binding material that the thread needs to be strong enough to withstand movement within the book, but not so thick that it bulks up the spine.

INFINITY BOOK
ANNE RIZK
This piece was designed as a blank binding to house material divided into two distinct sections. It takes as its starting point the concertina-fold page, but instead of simply binding this into two cover boards, two concertinas are cleverly bound at one end by single cover boards and at the other end into the two inside covers of a case-bound shell.

CAROUSEL BOOK
HEATHER WESTON
This carousel book, also known as a star book, is made by joining three separate, differently sized concertinas together. When closed it sits flat like a normal book, but when opened fully it forms a visually intriguing shape that looks like a carousel from the side and a star when seen from above.

PREPARING THE BOOK BLOCK

PREPARING THE GROUP OF PAGES THAT MAKES UP THE BOOK BLOCK—OR TEXT BLOCK—REQUIRES KNOWLEDGE OF A VARIETY OF BASIC TECHNIQUES. MASTERING THESE WILL HELP YOU CREATE A BOOK THAT WILL HOLD TOGETHER AND LAST.

PRACTICE

You may want to familiarize yourself with the techniques of preparing the book block by practicing on scrap paper. Save your practice pieces and use them to remind you of the steps as you move on to making and binding your own books.

SEE ALSO
Paper Grain, pages 10–11

**FLYING HIGH
HANNAH BROWN**
This card soft cover is wrapped around a single-section notebook using five stitches.

FOLDING

When folding paper for bookbinding use a bone folder to give a crisp edge.

1 Take one edge of the paper to the other edge. Press the bone folder into the center of the folded edge and move it outward, pressing firmly to flatten one half of the fold.

2 Return the bone folder to the center of the fold and run it over the other half of the fold, moving out from the center, creating a crisp edge all along. Use this technique when folding a single page (as shown) or several pages in a section.

ALIGNING THE BOOK BLOCK
The pages of the book need to be carefully aligned before binding.

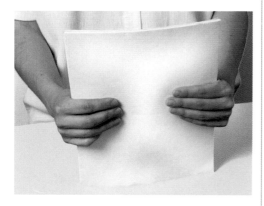

1 To create an evenly aligned stack of paper, jog the book block into alignment by tapping it firmly along the head of the stack, then along the foredge.

2 Handmade paper cannot be jogged easily because of its uneven deckled edge. In this instance, place each sheet on top of the one before, lining up the binding edge as closely as possible.

MAKING HOLES
To pierce holes in single sheets of paper—or a small number of pages—prior to stitching you can use a bookbinder's or embroidery needle, but to make holes in stacks of paper, or to make larger holes, use an awl.

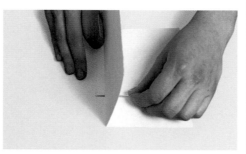

1 When using a needle, first mark the holes, then pierce each mark with the needle, pressing firmly but gently into the paper.

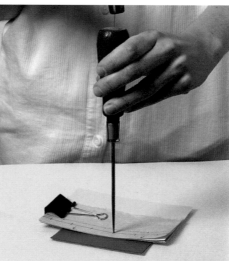

2 For larger holes or thicker stacks of paper, use an awl to punch the holes. Place a mat or card under the item to be punched to protect the work surface. Position the awl at a 90-degree angle to the book block, and hit the awl firmly with a hammer. Select a thicker awl for raffia, heavy cord, and leather thong bindings, and thinner awls for ribbon and thread bindings.

THE PARTS OF THE BOOK
Each part of the book has a specific name that you will see used throughout this chapter.

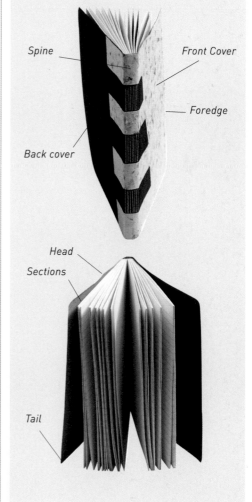

Spine, Front Cover, Foredge, Back cover, Head, Sections, Tail

SOFT AND HARD COVERS

SOFT OR HARD COVERS CAN BE USED TO CASE IN THE BOOK BLOCK. SOFT COVERS CAN BE MADE FROM CARD OR STURDY HANDMADE PAPERS, AND OFTEN HAVE A HOMECRAFTED LOOK AND FEEL. A HARD COVER IMPARTS A MORE FORMAL APPEARANCE TO A BOOK. IT PROTECTS DELICATE INSIDE PAGES AND HELPS TO KEEP THE BOOK CLOSED, SO MAY THEREFORE BE MORE SUITED TO A BOOK WITH MANY PAGES.

MAKING A SOFT COVER

A soft cover can be sewn into a single-section book block using pamphlet stitch (see page 82), or use the casing-in method described below to paste the cover to the book block.

1 To prepare a soft cover, first measure the dimensions of your book block, remembering to take into consideration the depth at the spine, which will need to be added to the length measurement.

HARD COVERS

To create a tougher stab-bound book, make a hinged front hard cover and a nonhinged back hard cover. Follow the principles used for making a hard cover, but replace the spine gap with a gap of ⅜in. (1cm) to form the hinge.

SEE ALSO

The Parts of the Book, page 79
Preparing the Book Block, pages 78–79
Single-section Binding, pages 82–84
Multisection Binding, pages 85–87

2 Mark these dimensions on the cover paper. Select a paper that is flexible enough to fold, but strong enough to withstand use.

3 Using a craft knife and ruler with a metal edge, trim the paper to the marked dimensions.

4 For a single-section book the cover paper can simply be scored and folded in half, using a bone folder to give a crisp crease. A cover for a thicker, multisection book will need to be scored in two places to accommodate the depth of the spine (right).

MAKING A HARD COVER

A hard cover can be used with books that are bound by any of the techniques described on pages 80–85.

1 Measure the front of your book block and transfer these measurements to a sheet of pasteboard, adding an extra ³⁄₁₆in. (5mm) at top, bottom, and foredge. Use these measurements and a craft knife to cut two pieces of pasteboard for the front and back covers. To measure the spine gap, position the front and back boards on the book block, allowing the spine of the book block to overhang the boards by about ³⁄₁₆in. (5mm). Wrap a strip of paper around the spine and mark on it the distance from the spine edge of the front cover to the spine edge of the back cover. This is how wide your spine gap should be.

2 Cut cover paper or book cloth to a size that encompasses both cover boards and the spine gap, plus an extra ³⁄₄in. (2cm) all around. Use a paste brush to apply paste or glue to the wrong side of the cover paper or cloth, working from the center out. Leaving enough space for the spine, carefully place the boards on the cover paper, making sure the tops and bottoms are straight and level. Diagonally trim off each corner of the cover material within about ³⁄₁₆in. (5mm) of the corner of the board. Use a metal ruler to carefully fold the long edges of the cover material over onto the boards.

3 Use a bone folder to tuck in the paper or cloth around each corner of the boards, then fold over the short edges and press down smoothly.

4 Run a bone folder along the outside of the spine to define the spine edges, then place the hard cover under a weight while it dries.

5 If you would like to apply a bookmark ribbon, cut it to one and a half times the height of the book's cover and glue in position with PVA glue.

6 Take your book block and, starting from the center and working out, apply paste to its front cover. Using both hands, carefully position the front of the book block on the inside of the case, ensuring that an even amount of cover edge shows all around. Smooth down.

7 Paste the book block's back cover in the same way and position onto the inside back cover of the case. You will need to lift the front cover at 90 degrees to allow the glued back page to reach the back cover. Place sheets of scrap paper between the case and the front and back pages to absorb moisture from the glue and place the book under a weight while it dries.

SINGLE-SECTION BINDING

A SINGLE-SECTION BOOK IS MADE UP OF A BATCH OF PAGES FOLDED AT THEIR CENTERS, WITH AN OUTER SHEET—SOMETIMES OF HEAVIER PAPER OR CARD—THAT ACTS AS THE SOFT COVER OF THE BOOK, OR THAT CAN BE PASTED TO THE INSIDE OF A HARD COVER.

PAMPHLET STITCH

Pamphlet stitch is based on three, five, or even seven holes—depending on the size of the book—and using it is one of the simplest methods of binding a single section. The thread can be hidden or visible as part of the design.

Pamphlet bindings can be fastened together with colored embroidery thread, cord, ribbon, raffia, and even shoelaces. Select a bookbinding or embroidery needle with a thickness similar to the thread to be used on the book. Thicker sewing materials, such as leather cord or heavy ribbon, will need a thicker needle with a larger eye.

CONSTRUCTING THE BOOK

Stack each page inside the next, and position the stack in the cover. The pamphlet stitch passes through all layers.

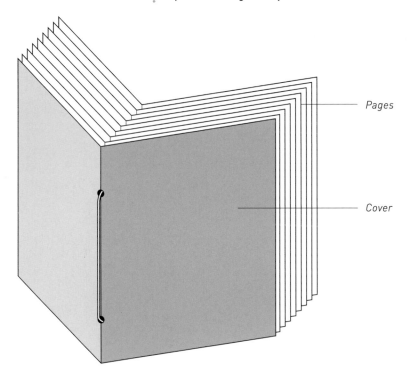

Pages

Cover

SEE ALSO
Preparing the Book Block, pages 78–79
Soft and Hard Covers, pages 80–81

THREE-HOLE PAMPHLET STITCH

A waxed embroidery or linen thread will pass through the holes easily.

1 Jog several sheets of paper into alignment and fold in half using a bone folder to create a sharp crease. Measure the center point along the fold and mark its position. Mark a hole on either side of the central mark to equally divide the spine along its length.

2 Pierce each of the three holes with a needle.

3 Thread the needle with colorful thread and begin stitching by pushing it through the center hole from the inside of the book.

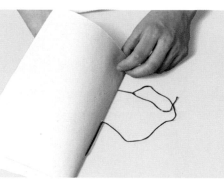

6 Insert the needle into the remaining hole, pull through to the inside, and pull taut.

7 Tie a double knot at the center of the stitching with the remaining thread and the tail from Step 4. Trim the thread with scissors, leaving ½in. (1.3cm) at the ends.

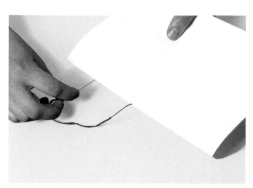

4 Pull the needle and thread out, leaving a tail of about 3in. (7.5cm) inside the book. Thread the needle into the top hole, pulling it through to the inside until taut.

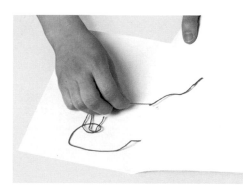

5 Push the needle through the center hole again and exit on the outside of the book. Pull the thread taut.

COMPLETED THREE-HOLE BINDING
The sewing can be reversed to create a decorative bow on the outside of the spine. Enter the center hole from the outside instead of the inside and follow the same order of stitches.

FIVE-HOLE PAMPHLET STITCH
This variation of the three-hole pamphlet stitch solidly anchors the pages of the section and adds more visual interest to the spine. Use the five-hole stitch when working with large pages that need greater stability, or when using the binding threads as decoration. Beading along the exterior spine looks especially effective.

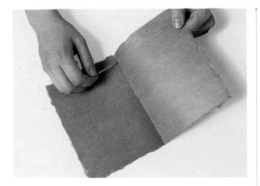

1 Prepare the book block and cover as for three-hole pamphlet stitch. Measure and mark five holes along the fold, including a center hole and two holes on either side that equally divide the spine along its length. Pierce the holes with a bookbinder's or embroidery needle.

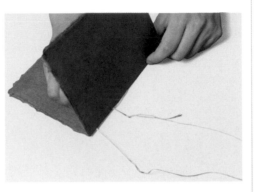

3 Push the needle through the end hole, from the inside to the outside of the book. Next thread through the hole just below the end hole, and pull the thread taut to the inside.

5 On the inside of the book, push the needle into the hole second from the end.

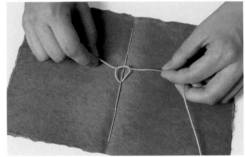

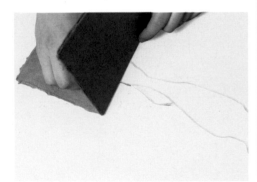

2 Thread the needle and pull it through the center hole, starting from inside the book. Push the needle through the hole just above the center hole next. Pull the thread taut and leave a tail of about 3in. (7.5cm) inside the book.

4 Bypass the center hole and thread through the next hole down from inside to outside. Push the needle through the end hole.

6 Thread through the center hole from the outside and pull the thread through. Tie a knot at the center hole. To hold the knot securely in place, tie a second knot over the first.

COMPLETED FIVE-HOLE BINDING
Increasing the number of holes for sewing through is a useful method as book sizes grow, so if you need to you can use the same sewing pattern with seven holes.

MULTISECTION BINDING

MULTISECTION BOOKS CAN BE THOUGHT OF AS SEVERAL SINGLE-SECTION BOOKS STITCHED TOGETHER AND STRENGTHENED WITH TAPES. A SOFT COVER CAN BE PASTED BENEATH THE SEWN TAPES, OR THE WHOLE BOOK CAN BE CASED-IN TO A HARD COVER.

USING TAPES

While bookbinding tape is an obvious material to use, the tapes can also take the form of decorative papers or ribbons, giving the bookbinder some attractive options for embellishing and decorating books.

SEWING ON TAPES

This multisection book is bound by two tapes. For a larger book, increase the number of tapes to anchor the sections and bind securely. Use waxed linen thread to ensure the sections are well secured.

1 Use a bone folder to fold 24 sheets of paper into six sections of four sheets each.

2 Stack the sections on top of each other on a flat surface. Place a weight on top of the pile of sections and leave for three to four hours to form a tight fold in each section.

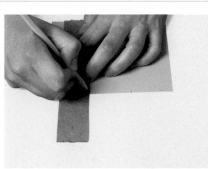

3 Cut a sheet of colored paper to the same length as the section spine. The paper does not have to be the same width, since it will be used for a template for piercing the holes. Measure the width of the tapes; in this case they are 1⅜in. (3.5cm) wide. Mark the placement of the first tape starting ½in. (1.3cm) from the top of the spine. Make a second mark 1⅜in. (3.5cm) from the first mark, indicating the width of the tape. Repeat the step for the second tape, making a mark ½in. (1.3cm) from the bottom of the spine and then 1⅜in. (3.5cm) from that mark, to indicate the width of the tapes. These four marks will show where to pierce the holes.

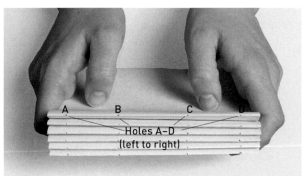

A   B   C   D
Holes A–D
(left to right)

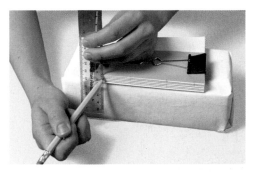

4 Clip the template to the stack of sections, ensuring that the sections and template are flush with the edge of the spine. Using a pencil and ruler, draw straight lines down the side of the spine, following the marks made on the template, to indicate the holes for piercing.

SEE ALSO

The Parts of The Book, page 75
Preparing the Book Block, pages 78–79
Soft and Hard Covers, pages 80–81
Single-section Binding, pages 82–84

5 Use a bookbinder's or embroidery needle to pierce the marked holes in each section. Thread a needle with waxed linen thread—in this instance a length of 30in. (75cm).

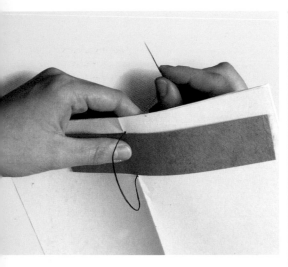

6 Take a single section and begin sewing by passing the needle through hole B from the inside. Exit hole B and enter hole A from the outside. Place the tape in position between the two holes as you pull the thread taut, to hold the tape in place.

7 Tie a double knot over hole B on the inside to secure the thread. Push the needle through hole C and exit to the outside of the section.

8 Place the second tape in position and pull the thread taut as you enter hole D.

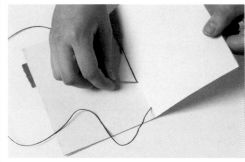

9 Pull the thread through hole C for a second time.

10 Place the next section on top of the first and push the needle through hole C of this new section.

11 Pull the needle through hole D to the outside and position the tape.

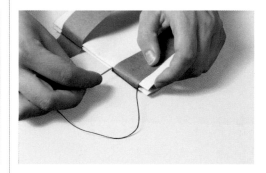

12 Enter hole C again and pull the needle through, pulling the thread taut.

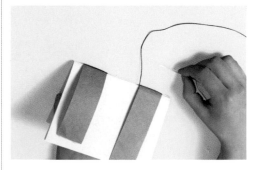

13 Pull the needle through hole B to the outside. Exit the section and loop the thread around the tape. Enter hole A to the inside of the section and exit through hole B.

14 Add the third section by entering hole B of the new section. Follow the same pattern to continue adding sections.

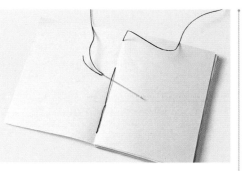

15 When all the sections are in place, tie a double knot flush with the center hole. Trim the ends of the knot to ½in. (1.3cm).

ADDING COVERS

The completed book can be pasted into a hard cover, following the steps on pages 78–79, or they can form part of the decorative appeal of a soft-cover book.

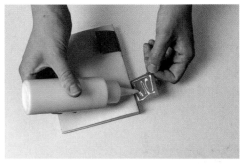

1 Cut covers for the front and back of the book, and apply PVA glue to the tapes at the front of the book.

2 Position the front cover beneath the tapes and press the tapes down. Repeat for the back cover.

COMPLETED TAPE BINDING
The binding is strong and durable, and the pages will lie flat when opened.

STAB BINDING

STAB BINDING, WHICH IS OFTEN REFERRED TO AS JAPANESE BINDING, IS TRADITIONALLY PAIRED WITH TWO SEPARATE COVERS AND SINGLE INNER PAGES. HARD COVERS CAN BE MADE WITH A PASTED HINGE, OR SOFT COVERS WITH A SCORED HINGE.

SEE ALSO

The Parts of the Book, page 79
Preparing the Book Block, pages 78–79
Soft and Hard Covers, pages 80–81

BINDING PATTERNS

The visible, decorative sewing along the spine gives this binding its characteristic appearance. Many different binding patterns exist, including the tortoiseshell and hemp leaf, each with its own unique story and rich heritage. The basic five-hole Japanese binding described here works well on books of all sizes.

FIVE-HOLE STAB BINDING

Since the binding and knotting are all external, it is a good idea to start with extra thread to avoid having to tie on a second piece midway through the stitch pattern. Five-hole binding usually requires thread five times the height of the book.

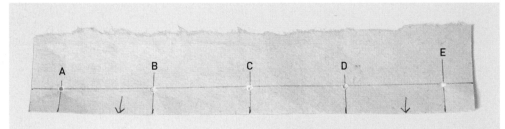

1 Create a template by trimming a piece of scrap paper to the length of the book's spine. Mark five holes ½in. (1.3cm) from the long edge of the spine, with a center hole and two holes on either side. Mark arrows on the template to indicate which is the spine edge.

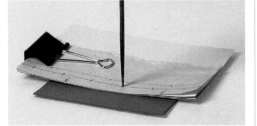

2 Align and stack single sheets of paper to prepare the book block. Here we are using handmade papers that form the pages and the cover. If you are adding a soft cover of heavier card, score a line on the card, ½in. (1.3cm) from the long edge of the spine. Clip the template to the stack of papers. Place the clipped stack on a protective surface and pierce the holes using an awl and hammer.

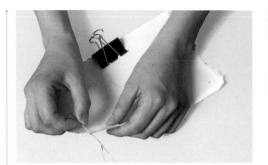

3 Thread a bookbinder's or embroidery needle with waxed thread, raffia, or ribbon. Here we are using a thin strand of raffia. Begin sewing by entering hole A from the back of the book and pulling through until a tail of 2in. (5cm) remains.

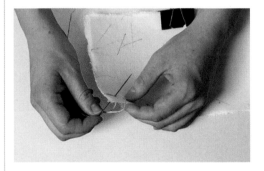

4 Loop the thread around the head of the book and enter hole A from the back. Loop the thread around the spine of the book and enter A for a third time. Pull taut.

5 Enter hole B from the front and pull the thread through to the back. Loop the thread around the spine of the book and enter hole B for a second time. Pull taut.

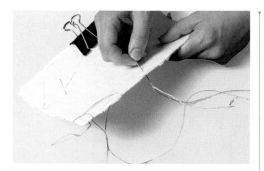

6 Enter hole C from the back and pull the thread through to the front.

7 Loop the raffia around the spine of the book and again enter hole C and pull taut.

8 Enter hole D from the front and pull the thread to the back. Loop the thread around the spine and enter hole D again, pulling the thread taut.

9 Enter hole E at the tail of the book from the back. Loop the raffia around the tail of the book and enter E again. Loop the raffia around the spine of the book and push through hole E for a third time.

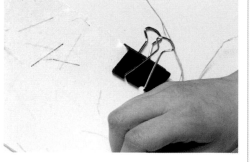

10 The next steps involve sewing back up to the head of the book, filling in the spaces left on the first pass. All sewing is now done from hole to hole, with no looping around the spine. Enter hole D from the front and pull to the back.

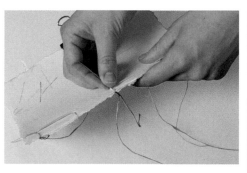

11 Enter hole C from the back and pull through. Enter hole B from the front and pull to the back.

12 Tie a double knot to secure the stitching.

THE COMPLETED FIVE-HOLE STAB BINDING
The stitch pattern holds the book in a strong bind, with a single length of thread achieving rigidity in the spine.

PROJECT

CONCERTINA BOOK

THE FOLDS OF THIS FUN CONCERTINA BOOK ALLOW THE FINISHED OBJECT TO BE HELD IN THE HAND AND READ LIKE A BOOK, BUT WHEN OPENED FULLY, THE SINGLE SHEET MAY BE SEVERAL FEET LONG.

SEE ALSO

The Parts of the Book, page 79
Preparing the Book Block, page 78–79
Soft and Hard Covers, pages 80–81

The concertina is made by repeated counterfolding of a sheet of paper, however you are not restricted to a single sheet, since a number of sections can be glued together, allowing you to increase the size of the book or add different papers.

FOLD LINES FOR THE CONCERTINA
The dotted lines indicate the marks on the underside of the sheet, while the solid lines show marks to be made on the top side.

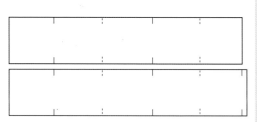

CONCERTINA BOOK
The concertina book has two distinct sides: the front, which is usually presented to the reader, and the back, which is often, although not always, left blank.

WHAT YOU WILL NEED

- Paper: one sheet 3¾ x 18¾in. (9.5 x 47.5cm) and one sheet 3¾ x 19¼in. (9.5 x 49cm), both with grain parallel to the short edge
- Pencil
- Metal ruler
- Bone folder
- PVA glue
- Paste brush
- Weight
- Craft knife
- Cutting mat
- Book cloth or cover paper: two pieces 6 x 6in. (15 x 15cm)
- Pasteboard: two sheets 4 x 4in. (10 x 10cm)
- Scrap paper

1 Take the shorter sheet of paper and use a pencil to mark the top and bottom of the sheet at intervals of 7½in. (19cm). Turn the sheet over and mark the back at the same intervals, but starting 3¾in. (9.5cm) in from the edge, so that the marks are positioned in between the marks on the other side. Repeat on the longer sheet of paper. You will be left with an extra portion of ½in. (1.3cm) at the end of the second sheet, which will become the flap used to join the two sheets together.

2 Use a bone folder along a metal ruler to lightly score between the points marked on the front of the first sheet, then turn it over to score between the marks on the other side. Repeat with the second sheet. This will ensure the paper folds easily and cleanly.

4 Lightly glue the inside of the short flap on the longer strip and join the two strips together so that the flap is behind the end of the shorter strip, and a mountain fold in the shorter strip follows the join. Dry the joint under a weight, then use a craft knife to trim any paper protruding at the top or bottom of the join.

6 Tuck in the corners then fold over the remaining two sides. Repeat Steps 5 and 6 for the second cover board, and dry both covers under a weight.

7 Fold the concertina book block and place a sheet of scrap paper under the top sheet. Apply glue to this top sheet, lightly but thoroughly.

3 Start with the shorter strip and fold the first crease backward, the next forward, and so on until all creases are folded. Repeat with the second strip of paper. Your score marks should end up on the inside each fold.

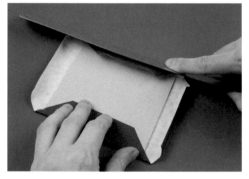

5 Starting from the center and working out, use a paste brush to apply PVA glue to the book cloth or cover paper, then place a sheet of pasteboard at the center. Cut off the four corners of the book cloth or cover paper and use a metal ruler to help fold the two opposite sides onto the pasteboard.

8 Pick up the glued end sheet of the concertina with both hands and lightly position it on the reverse of one of the hard covers. When you are sure it is central, firmly press in place. Repeat Steps 7 and 8 for the back cover.

QUILLING TOOLS
Quilling shapes can
be rolled by hand, or
using a split or needle
quilling tool.

DRAGONFLY
CECELIA LOUIE
Reminiscent of the
translucency of an actual
dragonfly's wings, the vellum
used as the background to
the quilling allows light to
pass through the wings and
illuminate the motifs. The
illumination is especially
unusual when viewed
through a window.

EQUIPMENT CHECKLIST
Here's what you will need to start
quilling.
- Quilling tool
- Cocktail sticks
- PVA glue
- Circle template
- Reverse-action tweezers
- Work board
- Cork or foam board, or
  corrugated cardboard with
  plastic wrap or wax paper
- Pins
- Pencil

UNIT 5

QUILLING

QUILLING IS THE ART OF ROLLING LONG, NARROW STRIPS OF PAPER INTO
ONE OF A NUMBER OF BASIC SHAPES, INCLUDING COILS, SCROLLS, AND
TEARDROPS—SOME OF WHICH ARE SQUASHED AND CREASED—AND APPLYING
THEM TO A BACKGROUND TO CREATE ABSTRACT OR FIGURATIVE DESIGNS.

HAVAS ANNUAL REPORT
YULIA BRODSKAYA
PHOTOGRAPHED BY
JOHN ROSS
This intricate quilling
design was developed for
Havas Media, a leading
global advertising and
communications services
group. This is one of four
artworks commissioned
for their annual report.
The artworks were
eventually used as posters
and the report itself was
printed on the back sides
of the posters.

The rolling is done either between the finger and thumb, or by using a special tool. Papers of different widths may be used, and different basic shapes require strips of varying lengths.

BRIEF HISTORY

It is believed that this papercraft may have originated in ancient Egypt, but the first clear reference to the art is in fifteenth-century England, where it was used by poor ecclesiastical organizations to provide backgrounds for religious sculptures, in imitation of the gold and silver filigree used by wealthier institutions. The art was revived in the seventeenth century by ladies of leisure, who used it to decorate workboxes, screens, and cabinets. It has gone out of style and been revived several times since, and like many papercrafts, it is currently enjoying a revival.

The origin of the name "quilling" is unclear. It could come from the quill pen, into whose split end a paper strip was inserted before being rolled, or from the porcupine quill, used as a needle by North American Indians when decorating moccasins with animal hair in a filigree manner.

PAPERS

Quilling paper strips are not only available in numerous shades and varying widths, but also in varying color treatments, including gradations, metallics, pearl, and two-tone. The most widely used width of strip, 1/8in. (3mm), is also the best choice for the first-time quiller. Cutting your own paper is also a fun and feasible way to add to your stash of strips, although this can be time-consuming and it is difficult to ensure exact widths.

EQUIPMENT

Quilling is made all the easier by the use of a quilling tool. There are two main types of tool, one has a split end, into which the end of the paper strip is trapped before it is rolled, while the other has a needle end around which you coil the paper strip.

A circle template is another useful accessory that allows you to create evenly sized coils, while reverse-action tweezers are invaluable for placing elements that are too small for fingers to reach, and can be used to hold pieces in place while you position other elements.

A good paper or craft glue, such as PVA, can be applied with a cocktail stick to the coiled shapes to keep them together, and the same glue is used to stick quilled motifs to their background.

SCENT
YULIA BRODSKAYA
Yulia used card and heavy paper for the quilling in this design, and she didn't use any specialist tools—just some cocktail straws and sticks. Using tools and materials in this free manner allowed her to "draw" with the paper, creating a very free image that conjures all types of smells and scent.

DECORATIVE DESIGNS
The core shapes (demonstrated over the page) can be incorporated into numerous projects, as shown in these flower and butterfly designs.

QUILLING SHAPES

THE QUILLING ARTIST HAS A BASIC PALETTE OF SHAPES TO BEGIN WORKING WITH, AND CAN USE KNOWLEDGE OF THESE TO CREATE MANY MORE MOTIFS.

PAPER STRIPS

The size of the shape you quill will depend on the length of paper strip and the size of the quilling tool. It is a good idea to practice making basic coils and other shapes using varying lengths of paper and recording the results, perhaps by sticking the shapes to a board to form a kind of sampler.

Tearing rather than cutting your paper strip to the right length produces a more subtle join on coils, since scissors create a sharp edge that will show when a coil is glued closed.

Tight coil

Loose coil

Eccentric coil

Crescent

Teardrop

Eccentric teardrop

Loose scroll

C-scroll

S-scroll

Asymmetric S-scroll

Marquise

Shaped marquise

Shaped teardrop

Heart

Eccentric coil heart

V-scroll

Asymmetric V-scroll

Asymmetric heart scroll

Heart scroll

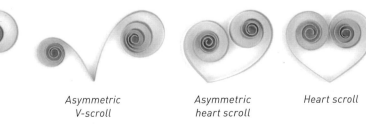

QUILLING ARTIST'S PALETTE

The quilling artist has a palette of 20 basic shapes to work with plus any other shapes that she may invent herself. More core shapes are formed by adapting the techniques used to make coils and scrolls.

COILS

The coil forms the basis of many quilled shapes.

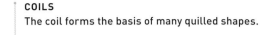

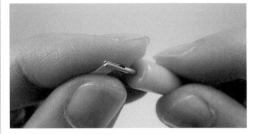

1 When using a slotted quilling tool, insert the end of the paper strip into the slit, lining up the edge with the tip of the tool to leave the smallest crimp possible. Turn the tool, keeping your finger against the paper to prevent unwinding.

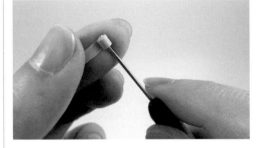

2 When using a needle tool, line up the end of the paper strip with the tip of the needle. Gently press the needle length against your finger, and using your thumb to rub against your index finger, roll the paper strip into a coil, leaving no crimp in the center.

3 Whether using a slotted or needle tool, keep the coil even using your index finger on top of the tool.

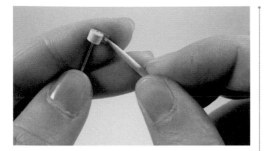

4 To create a tight coil, use a cocktail stick to dab a little PVA glue on the end to seal the coil before removing it from the tool.

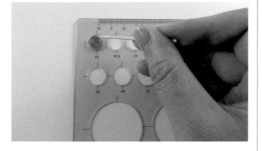

5 The coil can be allowed to loosen on the work surface to the desired size before gluing as above. To make loose coils of the same size, release the coil into a circle template and glue within its circumference.

6 To make an eccentric coil, use a pin to push all the coils to one end and to secure the coil to a cork or foam work board. Dab glue across all the strips and release when dry. The glue will be visible, so remember to turn this element over when arranging it into your design.

MORE SHAPES

Other shapes can be made by manipulating a basic coil.

1 To shape a teardrop, pinch one end sharply so the crease goes through each ring.

2 To shape an eye or marquise, pinch both ends at the same time, leaving no crimp in the center.

3 Push your thumbs in opposing directions to make a shaped marquise.

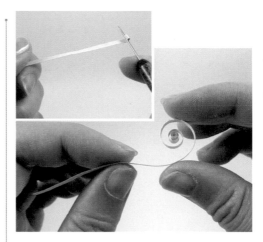

4 To create a loose scroll, lightly straighten a coil by drawing the tool along two-thirds of its length. Re-coil again with your fingers.

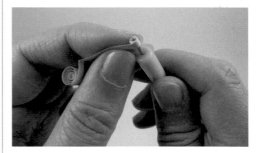

5 Fold the strip in half and curl the ends in the same direction to make a double scroll, or in the opposite direction to make a V-scroll.

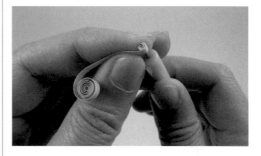

6 To make an S-scroll curl both ends of a strip in opposite directions.

QUILLING APPLICATIONS

WHEN PUT TOGETHER THE BASIC QUILLING SHAPES CAN BE INCORPORATED INTO ALL MANNER OF DESIGNS, AND APPLIED TO A WIDE RANGE OF SURFACES.

**HEART
CECELIA LOUIE**
A love for spring flowers is barely contained within the heart-shaped border, which was first pinned to a cork board to create a non-shifting corral.

QUILLED FLOWERS

Making these flowers and leaves will give you an idea of how you can use and combine the basic quilling shapes to create a larger overall design.

1 Make a loose coil for a flower center. Lightly mark the coil with five equally spaced lines that the petals will be positioned by.

2 To form the flower petals, mark a strip in four places along its length at equal intervals. The length of strip you use will determine how large your petals will be. Scrape the paper between your finger and a quilling tool, as you would with curling ribbon for gifts.

3 Fold along all the markings and use a cocktail stick to dab a little PVA glue on the first fold.

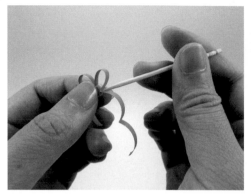

4 Match the glued fold to one of the markings on the flower center. Continue gluing and matching each fold up to each line on the flower center.

5 Finish by gluing both ends at the same time. This may be easier done by holding the ends with a pair of tweezers.

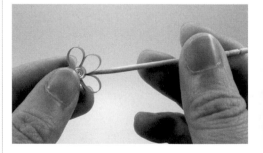

6 Use a cocktail stick to press each petal's fold firmly to the flower center to ensure it is glued securely.

7 Continue making more flowers as desired. While the glue is still wet, place the flowers on a flat surface and intermittently press gently to keep all quilled items even.

8 To make the leaves, make loose, V-scrolls, and S-scrolls (see page 94). Allow one coil of a V-scroll to extend past the other, and one end of the S-scroll to be larger than the other.

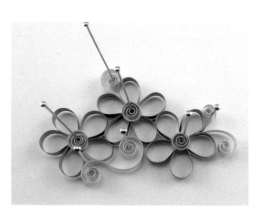

9 Experiment with arrangements of the flower and leaf elements on a work board, using pins as necessary to prevent them from moving.

COMBINING THE ELEMENTS

When you have made up the various elements, bring them together to form the completed design. You can do this by eye on your quilling board, trying different arrangements before gluing, or you can use a template—one of your own making, or from a book or the internet.

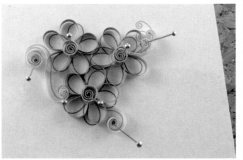

1 Place the template on a cork, foam, or cardboard work board, and cover with plastic wrap or wax paper. Place the elements in position over the template. You can use pins to keep them in place.

2 Put a little glue on the end of a cocktail stick and carefully slip it between two touching elements. Repeat with all touching elements.

CLEAN FOLDS

To make folds without marking the paper, line up the end of a strip to the desired length on the ruler, letting the excess overhang the "0" side of the ruler. Press down on that "0" edge, leaving a score line that can be followed up with a sharp fold that won't mark the strip.

GLUING TO THE BACKGROUND

1 Pour a little PVA glue onto a piece of scrap paper and smear across the paper to a width that matches that of your completed quilled design. Hold the design with tweezers and dip it into the shallow bath of glue. Lift and look for missed areas, and dip into the glue again if necessary.

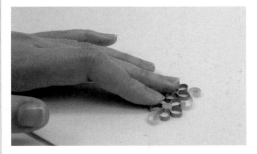

2 Place the design on the background, and gently press with fingertips to firmly attach all items.

VARIATION

Six teardrop shapes, with spirals facing in the same direction, make up the petals for this flower. A marquise makes the leaf, while the sprig is formed by applying a loose scroll to one-third of a strip, and scraping the remaining two-thirds to make the stem.

PROJECT

BUTTERFLY KEEPSAKE BOX

THE FINE, DELICATE NATURE OF QUILLING BELIES THE FACT THAT THIS DECORATION IS IN FACT SURPRISINGLY STRONG, AND AS SUCH YOU CAN USE QUILLING MOTIFS TO PERSONALIZE A VARIETY OF OBJECTS, INCLUDING A PLAIN BOX, A TENT CARD, OR A BOOK.

Make sure the final surface is porous so the glue will adhere securely. This paper-covered keepsake box will allow for proper bonding despite the shallow texture. A plastic or coated box would not be suitable since the glue would be unable to penetrate the surface.

WHAT YOU WILL NEED

- Quilling strips for the wing outline, all ⅛in. (3mm) wide:
  - 2 deep red strips, each 5¾in. (14cm) long
- Quilling strips for the upper wing fillers, all ⅛in. (3mm) wide:
  - 2 pink strips, each 4in. (10cm) long
  - 2 orange strips, each 4in. (10cm) long
  - 2 light green strips, each 1½in. (4cm) long
- Quilling strips for the lower wing fillers, all ⅛in. (3mm) wide:
  - 2 lilac strips, each 2¾in. (7cm) long
  - 2 light green strips, each 2¾in. (7cm) long
- Quilling strips for the head and antennae, all ⅛in. (3mm) wide:
  - 1 deep red strip, 1¼in. (3cm) long
  - 1 lilac strip, 2in. (5cm) long
- Pencil
- Cocktail sticks
- PVA glue
- Reverse-action tweezers
- Pins
- Quilling tool

BUTTERFLY KEEPSAKE BOX
A personalized box makes a wonderful gift, and decorating an object in this way allows the artist to express themselves in a practical and beautiful way. The finished piece can be further protected with several coats of clear varnish.

SEE ALSO

Quilling Shapes, pages 94–95
Quilling Applications, pages 96–97

TEMPLATE

This butterfly template may be scaled up or down to suit any project, and for this box is used at 100%. The template can be used as a visual guide to refer to occasionally as you form the butterfly, or you can place it on your work board and under some plastic wrap in order to work directly over it (see Combining the Elements, page 97).

1 Start by forming the wing outline using two deep red strips, each 5¾in. (14cm) long. From one end, fold at 1¾in. (4cm). Use a pencil and lightly mark 3in. (8cm). Gently curl the ribbon strip like you would with curling ribbon.

3 Dab a small dot of glue on the bottom half of one wing outline and fix the two wings together.

5 Fold an orange strip at 1¾in. (4cm) and quill into an asymmetric double scroll. Repeat for the opposite wing.

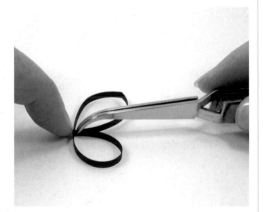

2 Use PVA glue applied with a cocktail stick to glue both ends of one wing perpendicular to the pencil mark to create the outline. Use tweezers to press the ends against the body, which can be held in place with either your finger or pins. Repeat with the second strip.

4 Fold each of the two pink strips at 2½in. (6cm). Use a quilling tool to gently curl each strip into an asymmetric heart scroll. Glue the fold of one heart scroll to the middle of the wing, and repeat on other side.

6 Quill a light green strip into a loose coil. Place in the tip of the upper wing. Repeat for the opposite wing.

7 Fold a lilac strip at ¾ in. (2cm) and 2in. (5cm). Gently curl the strip. Dab glue at the corner of the bottom wing and, working with one end at a time, glue the loops in place, adhering the folds into the corner last. Use pins to prevent shifting.

10 Ensure all touching areas are secured with glue to prevent movement, then glue the butterfly to the box, following the instructions on page 97. Add flowers of varying sizes with leaves and greenery as desired.

8 Fold a light green strip at 1¾ in. (4cm) and quill into an asymmetric double scroll. Glue in place next to the lilac loops. Repeat on the opposite lower wing.

9 For the head, gently curl the 1¼-in. (3-cm) long deep red strip in the middle until the ends touch. Dab a small amount of glue on the ends to secure them. Slip this teardrop shape between the two upper wings. Fold the 2-in. (5-cm) long lilac strip in half and curl into a loose V-scroll. Adhere the fold to the center of the teardrop.

THE COMPLETED BUTTERFLY

HANDMADE PAPERS
Papers made from recycled paper pulp or plant pulps usually have a textured quality that adds another dimension to woven art forms. See pages 142–151 if you would like to try making your own.

See pages 142–151

EQUIPMENT CHECKLIST
....
Weaving really lets the paper do the talking, but you will likely also make use of the following items:
- Pencil
- Craft knife
- Cutting mat
- Metal ruler
- PVA glue
- Masking tape
- Clear adhesive tape

UNIT 6

WEAVING

WEAVING WITH PAPER IS A TRULY VERSATILE CRAFT, NOT LEAST BECAUSE A VARIETY OF PAPERS CAN BE EFFECTIVELY WOVEN, AND THE PATTERN PERMUTATIONS ARE VAST. INTERWEAVING PAPER ALLOWS YOU TO CREATE SOME STRIKING DESIGNS, YET IT IS ONE OF THE SIMPLEST ART FORMS.

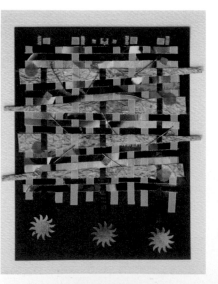

**PASSION
ELLEN JACKSON**
The plain weave technique can be used to create myriad effects by using various papers. Here a mix of cut handmade, shredded recycled, and commercial papers is used, with the strips taking on various widths and shapes to give great vibrancy and variety.

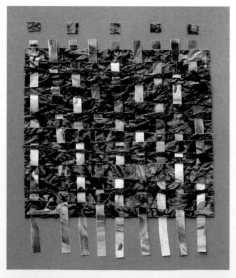

**SURFACE PLAY
ELLEN JACKSON**
Weaving can make use of a huge variety of papers, including plain or patterned handmade varieties, shredded recycled papers, and decorative giftwrap embellishments. Ellen Jackson has chosen papers that have a common color theme although she makes use of mixed patterns.

EXPERIMENT WITH PAPER
Many interesting weaves can be created using the innate qualities of paper. You can mix up different colors and textures for eye-catching results.

BRIEF HISTORY

Paper weaving is as old as paper. In China and, particularly later, in Japan, very narrow paper strips were woven to make bags, mats, and even clothes of great durability. In the 1960s several major textile manufacturers wove paper in a search for new, nonsynthetic fibers. For a short time paper fabric was available commercially, but never became popular.

PAPERS

All sorts of papers can be used for weaving, depending on the visual or textural effect you want to achieve. When you are starting out, practice using medium weights, but as you become confident you will want to experiment with the wonderful color of tissue and wrapping papers and the texture and three-dimensional possibilities of handmade papers. You can also recycle anything from glossy magazine pages and candy wrappers to old letters, maps, and manuscripts.

METHODS

The most basic method is to weave a warp (vertical strip) of one color and a weft (horizontal strip) of another in a "one under, one over" pattern, to produce a checkerboard effect. The number of "unders and overs" can go through many mathematical permutations to create woven patterns of great intricacy.

Traditional paper weaves used paper that was twisted before being woven, but paper can also be woven flat, as strips. The strips need not be of equal width or be straight-edged. For example, identically sized but differently colored squares of paper can each be cut randomly into strips, then woven together in strict order to create a tipsy checkerboard effect.

Parallel-edged strips need not be woven flat. At intervals, the strip may loop out of the weave before being tucked in again, rather like a piece of knitted yarn caught on a nail. Arranged in patterns and at set heights, this can create beautiful relief patterns.

PINK/BLACK ROYALE ELLEN JACKSON
In a variation on the three-dimensional weave, strips of patterned handmade paper are woven in and out of slits cut into a single sheet of handmade paper, and arranged to stand proud of the surface.

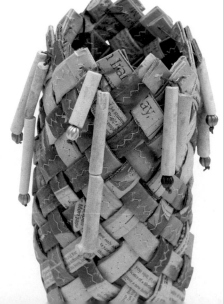

NEWSPAPER VASE ANNE WILLITTS
Anne has designed a three-dimensional vessel woven from strips of tightly folded and machine-stitched sheets of newspaper. The edge is finished with fragments of old clay tobacco pipes gathered from the river Thames foreshore in London.

WEAVING DESIGNS

IT IS POSSIBLE TO ACHIEVE A WEALTH OF INTERESTING EFFECTS BY WEAVING TOGETHER FLAT STRIPS OF PAPER.

DESIGN OPTIONS

The "one under, one over" pattern is the easiest of all weaves, but this does not mean it has to be boring. For example, the warp and weft strips need not be the same width, and they can both be varied to create an undulating color effect across the surface of the weaving. Alternatively, this form of regular pattern can be varied to create a multitude of designs, since a strip can be placed in front of or behind any number of crossing strips. On the reverse side, the pattern is the same, but the colors are reversed.

Paper may also be woven three-dimensionally, where parallel-edged strips can be creased to stand upright, forming ledges that catch the light.

SEE ALSO
Creasing and Cutting, pages 12–13

PLAIN WEAVE

The "one under, one over" pattern repeats every two rows and appears staggered, like brickwork. You can vary the width of the warp and weft strips, or use paper with a deckle edge for a soft effect.

1 The warp (vertical) strips can be made from a sheet of paper that is kept intact at the top. Make a number of vertical cuts at regular intervals across the sheet, each one starting about ½in. (1.3cm) down from the top of the sheet. Cut your weft strips out of a completely different sheet of paper.

2 Starting at the top, weave the first weft strip over the first warp strip, under the second, over the third, and so on to the last warp.

3 Weave the second weft strip under the first warp strip, over the second, under the third, and so on. Repeat Steps 2 and 3 with the remaining weft strips.

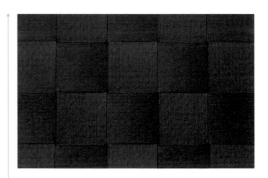

4 To keep the weave straight and tight, make sure you push each weft tight up to the previous one. You may like to glue the strips in place, by putting a dab of PVA glue where it can't be seen at each end.

5 If necessary, trim the edges to neaten.

TEARING STRIPS

If you are looking for a less rigid, more uneven effect, you may want to try tearing your paper strips instead of cutting with a craft knife. It is difficult to tear the warp threads and keep the top portion of the paper sheet intact, so a slightly different approach needs to be taken.

1 Tissue paper is easy to tear, and weaving it increases its strength. Decide on the width of strips you would like to use, then fold the edge of the paper over a metal ruler and tear down. Repeat until you have all the strips you need.

2 Arrange the warp strips together on the work surface, then weave the weft strips through to your chosen pattern. Push up the weft strips with a craft knife where necessary to keep the weaving tight. Once finished, secure the ends of the warp and weft threads with clear tape.

IRREGULAR WEAVE

Irregular weaves are mathematical variations of the plain weave, and the permutations are endless. Some well-known ones are the zigzag, the patchwork, and the shadow blocks weave.

1 Cut your pieces as for plain weave. Weave the first weft by passing over the first two warps, then under the next two and over the next two.

2 Weave the second weft under one warp, over one, under one, and so on.

3 Continue following the same sequence from Step 1, until the weave is complete. Glue and trim if required as with plain weave.

4 Now weave the fourth weft over one warp, under one, over one, and so on.

5 Continue following the same sequence from Step 1, until the weave is complete. Glue and trim if required—as with the plain weave.

ENDLESS VARIATIONS

It is clear to see that the choice of variations on an irregular pattern could go on forever. With an artist's eye and skill, woven paper becomes a work of art.

TUMBLING BLOCK WEAVE

This flat weave pattern gives the effect of three dimensions. Follow this pattern to create an effective tumbling blocks motif, then use your experience to recreate your own ideas.

The orange warp is 6½ x 4½in. (16.5 x 11.5cm) wide, with six vertical strips, ¾in. (2cm). Six yellow weft strips are 6in. (15cm) long and ¾in. (2cm) wide. From the right, weave the wefts for the first row over one warp, under one, then over two, then under one and over one to finish. For row two, begin over two warps, under one, then over two again, and under one. For the third row, start under one, then over two, under one, and finally over two. Repeat rows one to three to form rows four to six.

WOVEN PATTERN
PAUL JACKSON

Patterned papers or images can be interwoven to give a whole new dimension to this papercraft. Striking or humorous effects can be achieved by interweaving two identical photographs, one slightly offset from the other, or two geometric patterns, two words, two old letters, two maps, and so on. The process may sometimes be a little painstaking, but the results are frequently very beautiful. To achieve this complex image, two reproductions of the same op art image were woven together, but with one slightly offset from the other.

1 Make eight red strips ½ x 6in. (1.3 x 15cm). Fold one end of each strip to a point to make it easier to weave.

2 Beginning at the top left corner, weave a red strip over the first warp and under the second weft, holding the main weave as you do so.

3 Turn the weave over and weave the second red strip under the third warp from the right to emerge between the second warp and the third weft.

4 Continue weaving strips from the top to form a gradually evolving pattern of blocks. Keep turning your work over to pull ends through.

5 Glue and trim the edges as for plain weave to complete the three-dimensional effect.

THREE-DIMENSIONAL WEAVE

With this pattern folds made in the warp and weft strips project from the surface of the flat weave and create a three-dimensional effect that works well on wall-hangings. Hang the piece opposite a natural light source and the projections will cast interesting shadows that change as the sun moves across the sky.

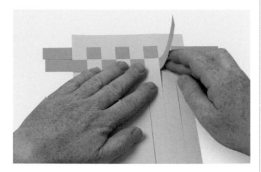

1 Cut the desired amount of warp and weft strips, and begin work as for basic weave. When you reach a point where you would like a projection to be, fold the strip back over the preceding warp and crease.

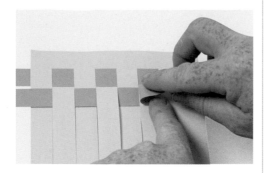

2 Curl the loose end of the weft back on itself, creating a fold that touches the opposite edge of the adjacent warp strip, then fold it back the opposite way, to give two valley folds and one mountain that form a raised triangle.

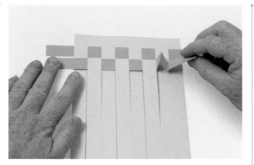

3 Weave the end of the weft strip under the next warp along, leaving the folded area projecting from the surface of the weave.

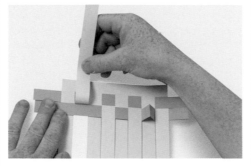

4 Repeat the folding technique described in Step 2 on a warp strip to make a warp projection.

5 Continue making projections in your preferred pattern.

6 Check that all the projections are standing up before gluing and trimming the loose ends as for basic weave.

DOODLE WEAVE
PAUL JACKSON

Once you have mastered the basics of paper weaving you can play with the principles to design more creative artworks. For this doodle weave two identical squares were sliced into irregularly shaped strips, one vertically the other horizontally, then woven together using the "one over, one under" technique.

PROJECT

WOVEN PAPER BOWL

THIS WOVEN PAPER BOWL LOOKS
ESPECIALLY EFFECTIVE WHEN MADE
TO MATCH THE PAPER NAPKINS OF
THE TABLE SETTING. IN THIS WAY
ANY BOWL CAN BE CUSTOMIZED
TO SUIT ANY EVENT, INCLUDING
BIRTHDAYS AND ANNIVERSARIES.

The bowl in this project is made using three
paper napkins from three different 3-ply
napkin sets, 13 x 13in. (33 x 33cm), but a great
deal of variety can be woven using just two
different colors or patterns, or combining
tissue paper or other malleable papers. This
bowl is plain on the outside and patterned on
the inside, however, you can choose to reverse
this method of work, or use pattern on both
sides, or intersperse pattern and plain on the
inside and out. Miss out the molding stage
and the same technique can be used to
make tablemats.

WHAT YOU WILL NEED

- Tablecover paper
- 3 paper napkins, 1 plain and 2 with
  different patterns
- Craft knife
- Cutting mat
- Metal ruler
- Wallpaper paste
- PVA glue
- Paste brush
- Glue stick
- Thumbtacks
- Cork board
- Iron
- Shallow bowl for molding
- Plastic wrap
- Acrylic varnish and paintbrush (optional)

BOWL SELECTION
ANNE WILLITTS

When choosing the napkins
to weave with, consider
how the colors and patterns
will work together and
complement each other.
The act of weaving creates
a whole new pattern.

1 Cut two squares of tablecover paper using one napkin as a template.

3 Paste one patterned layer of napkin onto one tablecover square.

4 Turn over and paste a plain napkin layer on the other side of the square. Repeat the process with the other patterned napkin, pasting a plain layer on the back as before. Leave to dry. Use a glue stick to glue down any unstuck edges.

2 Peel off the top patterned layer from each of the two patterned napkins, and separate the three layers of the plain napkin. Mix wallpaper paste with water and add a couple of tablespoons of PVA glue. The paste should be of a spreadable, creamy consistency, and not too thick.

5 Use a craft knife and metal ruler to cut each layered square into 12 strips of 1in. (2.5cm) wide, and two strips of ½in. (1.3cm) wide, giving 24 wide strips and four narrow strips in all, and making full use of the napkin size.

7 Gently flip alternate strips to the top of the board and place a dab of glue from the glue stick on each warp strip left on the board where the crossways weft strip will go.

9 Lift the warp strips down to stick over the weft and flip the next set of warp strips back to the top of the board.

6 For the warp, choose 12 wide and two narrow strips. Using thumbtacks, pin each strip at its very top edge to a cork board, so that the strips hang down side by side. Alternate or intersperse the two types of pattern, and include the narrower strips as desired to give some variety. Keep the plain sides face down on the board.

8 Carefully place the first weft strip, plain side down, over the warp strips close to the thumbtacks, and stick down. Add a touch of glue on the weft strip where each warp strip will be brought down to form the weave.

10 Repeat Step 8 to lay and stick the second weft/strip. Continue weaving and sticking down, making sure the warp and weft strips lie neatly together until they form a square. As with the warp, alternate or interperse the two types of pattern, and include the narrower strips as desired for variety. There may be one or two unused strips. Leave to dry. Trim the edges and iron flat.

11 Prepare a mix of wallpaper paste and PVA glue as in Step 1 and use a soft, wide brush to apply the paste all over the patterned side of the woven square. Line a shallow bowl with plastic wrap.

13 Cut off the excess paper at the top, rounding the edge, but leaving about ¾in. (2cm) of paper above the bowl edge.

14 When dry, remove the paper bowl from the mold. Glue the ¾in. (2cm) of paper edging onto the outside of the woven paper shape, to reinforce and neaten the top. Alternatively, trim off the extra paper all round the top to leave a smooth, cut edge.

12 Carefully lay the woven piece, paste side up, in the bowl and gently press and brush it against the sides, applying more paste as needed. The paper will gradually soften and can be eased into the shape of the bowl. Take care not to tear the damp strips at this stage. Use your fingers to smooth down creases at the edge.

WOVEN PAPER BOWL
Applying acrylic varnish to the bowl will make it sturdier, and the bowl can be further decorated by sticking on buttons or toning ribbon, if desired.

UNIT 7
PAPER CUTTING

PAPER CUTTING TECHNIQUES CAN BE USED TO CREATE FIGURATIVE OR ABSTRACT SHAPES FOR DECORATIVE PURPOSES, AS WELL AS FOR MAKING MOBILES AND COLLAGES. UNLIKE DECOUPAGE, WHERE ALREADY PRINTED MOTIFS ARE CUT OUT, PAPER CUTS ARE DERIVED FROM SHEETS OF BLANK COLORED PAPER—OR OVERALL PATTERNS—FOLLOWING DESIGNS BASED ON TRADITION OR EVOLVED BY THE PAPER CUTTERS THEMSELVES.

BALLOON CITY
BÉATRICE CORON

Béatrice Coron's series of "Personal Cities" began with the idea of imagining a city that would contain all the essential elements of a single person's life. Béatrice asked friends to describe the kind of city they would like to call home, then made a paper-cut image of each person's wishes. Balloon City draws its inspiration from the "floating world" (ukiyo), a prominent concept in Edo-period Japan, and the notion of the "green footprint." The floating world resonates with modern life in its depiction of a pleasure-oriented society and its analogy to mobility and global-village mentality. The green footprint is about being light on the planet and leaving no carbon footprint, and the artist here imagines how we could leave the planet for gardens and reorganize our communities off the ground.

HIDDEN SUMMER
LIZZIE THOMAS
Lizzie Thomas uses detailed cutting techniques to create a pocket-sized paper season. Murano paper is cut into tree motifs, with folded paper in between the cut pieces used to build up a fan, all housed in a pop-up hinged hardwood box. Lizzie was inspired by experiencing how the Japanese celebrate the seasons, and chose to use the delicate character of paper to represent the transience of nature.

BRIEF HISTORY

Decorative paper cuts dating from AD 207 have been found in northern China, and it is thought that the Chinese were cutting paper long before that. Paper cutting is also a tradition in Japan, Mexico, Poland, Germany, Switzerland, the Netherlands, and in areas of Dutch influence in the United States, such as Pennsylvania.

Originally, paper cuts were connected with religious and ceremonial observances, but when paper became more plentiful paper pictures were pasted on walls, furniture, and windows to brighten up the home. The cutters depicted familiar flowers and animals, and illustrated stories and legends.

In the late nineteenth century the cutting of paper portraits became popular in Western countries, and itinerant artists cut sometimes very humorous silhouettes of individuals and family groups. Silhouette cutting was a popular home hobby, but declined with the development of photography.

Today paper cutting is used extensively by graphic artists and illustrators and appears in magazines and travel brochures, and on posters and shopping bags. Keeping an eye on such work is a useful way to glean fresh ideas of your own.

PAPERS

All sorts of paper types can be used to great effect when it comes to paper cutting. Fine art paper is a favorite since it cuts very cleanly, is of a good thickness, and is available in a great range of colors. Handmade papers can tear when cut, but make excellent translucent and textured backgrounds on which to mount more delicately cut pieces. Recycled papers such as book pages or maps, origami papers, and translucent papers are just a few of the other possibilities.

THE GOLDEN SEA, IT HAS TEETH
PATRICK GANNON
Japanese mythology barely mentions the shark, so Patrick created his own "shark god." The temple on the jutting rock adds a sense of scale, but also enhances the piece's religious and mythological atmosphere. Patterned chiyogami paper forms the major element, and the pattern adds a sense of cultural context. Patrick cuts intricate designs with a craft knife, and makes use of layering techniques to weave the various elements over and under each other to create a sense of depth.

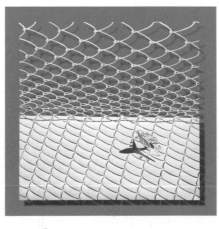

THE BIRD THAT THINKS IT'S A PLANE
BOVEY LEE
Handmade from mulberry tree bark, the rice paper that Bovey Lee cuts is tissue-thin, dense, and soft to the touch. It is backed with silk to add resilience, and hand cut with a knife. Color is not added to the off-white rice paper, so light play and shadow are essential to the overall impact of the image. The theme of self-perception is explored in this cutout, which cleverly features a bird that casts a shadow of a jumbo jet.

PAPER CUTTING TECHNIQUES

PAPER MAY BE CUT WITH SCISSORS OR A CRAFT KNIFE, EACH TOOL PROVIDING SLIGHTLY DIFFERENT EFFECTS. THESE TOOLS ARE USED WITH GREAT EFFECT IN A NUMBER OF STYLES, FROM DETAILED, INTRICATE WORK TO LAYERING EFFECTS AND SILHOUETTE.

The technique for cutting with scissors is to hold the paper in the air, grasp the scissors firmly with one hand and move the paper into the blades with the other. In this way, smooth curves result. Sharply angled corners are cut with the tip of the scissors. The paper can be a single sheet or may be folded to produce symmetrical cutouts.

If using a craft knife the blade must be sharp and the paper should rest on a resilient surface, and several layers may be stacked to cut multiples all at once.

SUN CITY
BÉATRICE CORON

Part of the artist's "Personal Cities" series (see page 112), Sun City was created for sun lovers. Coron works with DuPont's Tyvek high-density polyethylene fibers that though very strong are easy to cut. She starts by sketching a rough design on the white side of one sheet. She then adds two more sheets underneath the first, holding them together with adhesive tape (each sheet is cleaned and refined individually, and numbered one to three from top to bottom). Using a fine-point X-acto 11 blade, she cuts through all three sheets, cutting details and variations as she works.

CUTTING DIFFERENT PAPERS

It is useful to understand how different papers react to cutting.

Fine art paper such as Murano cuts very cleanly with a craft knife.

Handmade papers can be more difficult to cut if they are coarse grained. When using a craft knife they cut well in one direction, but tend to tear easily in the other direction, so are not suitable for delicate cutting. However, they can be cut into simple shapes, using scissors rather than a craft knife, and work well when cutting symmetrical shapes.

Recycled papers can be used to create unique paper cuts. These can be very delicate, so take extra care with a craft knife or sharp scissors.

Origami paper can be fun to cut because the patterns and colors instantly give the piece an exciting finish. These papers tend to be very thin, so again extra care must be taken: the sharper your blade, the better. Work from the inside to the outside when cutting a piece to minimize tear (see Detailed Shapes, page 116), or use sharp embroidery scissors.

Translucent papers such as vellum paper or tracing paper can be more difficult to cut but make excellent backgrounds when creating shadow silhouettes. Use scissors.

SYMMETRICAL CUTTING

Folding paper allows you to cut multiple, identical shapes.

1 Fold a strip of paper over and then over again. Here the strip is 16in. (40cm) long and 2½in. (6cm) high, so the final folded surface is 4in. (10cm) long and 2½in. (6cm) high.

2 Draw your design onto the surface. You will need to include a feature at either end that will join this piece to the next piece. In this example the elephant's tusks and tail are the joining features.

3 Carefully cut around the shape. Sharp embroidery scissors are used to cut out this delicate handmade paper.

4 Carefully unfold your piece to create a chain of symmetrical shapes. To create chains with more than four shapes, use a longer strip of paper and simply increase the amount of times you fold it over.

DETAILED SHAPES

Detailed shapes are most often cut with a craft knife, using one of two approaches, either working from the inside out, or working within a contained shape from the outside in.

1 Depending on how confident you are, either draw your shape with pencil first and use an eraser to remove pencil marks at the end, or cut freehand either from memory or working from a drawing or photograph.

2 Cut from the edge of your paper sheet to the body of the shape to be cut, in this case the trunk of the tree. Carefully cut around the shape, following the drawn lines if using.

3 Put pressure on the trunk with your finger to hold it in place while you cut the branches, working out from the trunk.

4 When working from the outside in, begin by cutting your outline. In this instance the outline of the tree shape is cut in the shape of a wine glass.

5 Work inward inside this contained shape, cutting out diamond-like shapes using a craft knife. Consider the design of the tree and cut out shapes of slightly differing sizes and positioned at slightly different angles to give a natural effect and the feel of movement.

6 Continue cutting shapes out, leaving a spine in the center as the tree trunk.

LAYERING

Layering techniques can yield varying results, based on the techniques used.

1 To create a scene such as a landscape or cityscape, choose several colors of paper to layer up. Cut out the fore-, mid-, and background pieces, remembering that elements in the foreground will be larger than the background images.

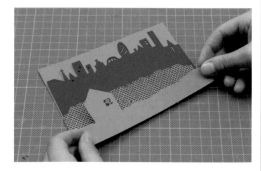

2 Layer the paper cutouts on top of each other to check the arrangement, then glue in place using PVA glue.

THE COMPLETED LAYERED CUT

The patterned paper is revealed through the cut details of the top layer.

3 For a different effect using a layering technique, cut out an outside shape, such as the outline of this Japanese-style fish, then work inward to cut out the details, such as the scales.

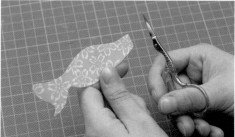

4 Draw around the outline of the fish onto a patterned paper, in this case origami paper, and cut this out using sharp embroidery scissors.

5 Use PVA glue to stick the top paper-cut fish onto the patterned paper.

SHADOW SILHOUETTING

The traditional silhouette paper cut can be brought up to date with the use of an interesting background paper.

1 To create a shadow silhouette, choose a translucent paper, such as vellum paper or a handmade paper, as a background. Cut out the silhouette from a colored paper: the darker the color, the more striking the silhouette.

2 Mount the silhouette onto the background using PVA glue. Use sparingly to avoid buckling.

3 Shine a light behind the piece to reveal the full effect, or turn it around to create a shadow silhouette.

PAPER-CUT WINDOW HANGING

FOLLOWING THESE STEPS YOU CAN MAKE YOUR OWN PAPER-CUT SCENE TO HANG IN A WINDOW. THIS PROJECT WAS INSPIRED BY A GERMAN PAPER CHRISTMAS DECORATION. THE FINISHED PIECE SHOULD BE HUNG IN A WINDOW THAT DOES NOT GET TOO MUCH DIRECT SUNLIGHT TO AVOID WARPING, OR ALTERNATIVELY CAN BE MOUNTED IN A CLEAR FRAME AND POSITIONED ON A WINDOWSILL.

WHAT YOU WILL NEED

- 3 sheets of art paper of different colors, here Murano paper has been used
- 1 sheet of translucent paper, such as a thin handmade paper or vellum paper
- Pencil
- Scissors
- Craft knife
- Cutting mat
- Drawing compass
- Eraser
- PVA glue
- Paintbrush
- Needle and thread

SEE ALSO

Paper Cutting Techniques, pages 114–117

PAPER-CUT WINDOW HANGING
This project could also be made using just one or two layered pieces of paper for a simpler effect, or try using four pieces for a more complex scene. The circle radius can also be adapted to create larger or smaller hanging scenes.

1 Use a drawing compass to draw a circle with a radius of 4in. (10cm) on each of the three sheets of art paper. Cut out using scissors.

2 To create the foreground, draw the landscape and tree outline on one of the circles. Use a compass to create a lip ⅜in. (1cm) from the edge of the circle by setting it to 3⅝in. (9cm).

3 Use a craft knife to cut around your pencil lines. Erase any leftover pencil lines, then cut shapes out of the tree as described in Detailed Cutting, page 116.

4 Repeat Steps 2 and 3 with the middle layer, this time drawing in a smaller house motif and making the lip width ½in. (1.3cm) in from the edge of the circle by setting the compass to 3½in. (8.7cm).

6 Draw around one of the circles onto the translucent paper and cut out.

8 Accessorize with individual cut pieces, such as the individually cut silhouette of a girl with a kite used here.

5 Repeat again with the background layer, this time making sure the solid tree motif is smaller again, and that the lip width is ⅝in. (1.6cm) from the edge of the circle by setting the compass to 3⅜in. (8.4cm).

7 Glue the layers together, starting with the translucent piece at the back and working your way forward to build up the scene. To help keep the piece flat as the glue dries, it can be useful to sandwich it between some heavy books.

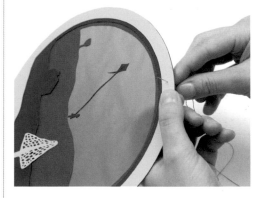

9 Either mount the piece in a clear frame, or using a needle and thread, carefully create a loop through the top of the circles so you can hang the piece up in a window or on a light box.

EQUIPMENT CHECKLIST

A minimal amount of equipment is needed for basic collage procedures; in most cases general art and craft equipment is all that is required.

- Pencil
- Craft knife (optional)
- Cutting mat
- Metal ruler
- Scissors
- Glue (PVA glue or wallpaper paste are most commonly used, although you can also use glue sticks or pens for delicate work)
- Paintbrushes
- Brayer (small roller)
- Watercolor paints (optional)
- Linseed oil and cloth (optional)

UNIT 8

COLLAGE

COLLAGE IS AN EXCITING AND VERSATILE PAPERCRAFT THAT DOES NOT REQUIRE MUCH IN THE WAY OF TECHNICAL SKILLS, JUST AN APPRECIATION OF SHAPES, TEXTURES, AND COLORS.

**KYLESKU, SUTHERLAND
ANN DAVIDSON**
This collage has a three-dimensional feel, since areas of it are not stuck down entirely. The unstuck pieces overlap and conceal some glued areas, and cast shadows onto them for added depth. The artist creates her collage elements by letting paint flow over wet paper and tearing around the most appealing sections. Collage lends itself well to evoking austere landscapes, like that of Kylesku, a hamlet in the Scottish Highlands. Watercolor washes convey the envelopment of mist and rain.

USEFUL TOOLS

The paper elements of your collages can be cut with scissors or a craft knife, or torn by hand, depending on the effects you are looking to achieve. Use pencils to plan compositions, marking lightly where you wish to place various elements, and use paintbrushes to apply glue or for painting collage pieces or backgrounds.

BRIEF HISTORY

The use of paper collage as an art form was pioneered in the twentieth century by artists such as Pablo Picasso and Henri Matisse. They cut and pasted paper shapes and added them to their paintings. Matisse went on to create pure collage pieces with no painting at all. Since then, many artists have looked to the versatility of paper to help them create their artwork.

PAPERS

Collage can make use of a variety of papers, ranging from commercial or handmade papers to recycled papers such as newsprint, postage stamps, and bus tickets. However, remember that the type, weight, and appearance of the papers can drastically alter the effect of the finished work. For example, layers of fine, transparent paper will create a delicate effect, whereas heavier corrugated cardboard and brown paper would give a more functional, industrial feel to a collage. As a general rule, heavy, textured paper will lead to bold effects; thin papers result in a lighter finish.

The simpler the imagery, the more imaginative you can be with the use of various papers. A piece of work can become busy and overcrowded if it includes lots of different types of paper.

METHODS

Once the basics of cutting, tearing, layering, and exposing have been mastered, in the world of collage it is almost impossible to make mistakes. Sections of the collage can be made separately but not incorporated immediately, while you make decisions on composition and content. Elements can be moved, added to, changed, or discarded.

Wallpaper paste and PVA glue are suitable for most collage projects. Wallpaper paste should be mixed with water to a thin consistency. PVA glue can be used undiluted, or if preferred it can by watered down to a creamy consistency.

THE ROCKS OF LOCH LAXFORD, SUTHERLAND
ANN DAVIDSON

In order to judge the composition of the image from a distance, Ann uses a removable adhesive tape to stick the pieces to a vertical surface, and makes changes as necessary. Numbered registration marks ensure the final composition is retained when removing the tape prior to gluing the pieces to backing paper. The method allows the artist a degree of control and precision. The limited palette helps to convey a remote landscape.

CUTTING AND PASTING

COLLAGE IS AN INCREDIBLY CREATIVE AND ADAPTABLE TECHNIQUE. YOU CAN ACHIEVE A WIDE VARIETY OF EFFECTS BY VARYING THE WAY IN WHICH YOU USE YOUR PAPER PIECES TO MAKE SHAPES AND PATTERNS.

A GALE IN STRATH FLEET, SUTHERLAND ANN DAVIDSON

Ann Davidson often creates her own colored paper by pouring paint onto wet paper and letting the paint flow, in a technique she refers to as "controlled accident." The various collage pieces are made by tearing away the areas she likes best. In this instance the paint dried into the shapes of birch trees, so she choose to compose a landscape around them.

CUTTING AND TEARING

The two basic methods of creating shapes for collage are cutting and tearing. Cutting is more precise, offering a quick way of making complicated shapes and patterns. The hard, clean edges that cutting produces would work well in a geometric abstract design or an architectural cityscape.

Tearing in a controlled fashion can create simple images, and with a little practice you can gain more control over the resulting shapes. Papers can be torn with or against the grain. It is slightly harder to work against the grain, and it requires more control to produce definite shapes. If a "straighter" edge is needed you must tear along the grain.

> **SEE ALSO**
>
> Paper Grain, pages 10–11
> Creasing and Cutting, pages 12–13

CUTTING

Cutting can be carried out using scissors or a craft knife. Scissors are easier to handle but may not allow the degree of accuracy afforded by a knife blade. Keep your fingers clear of the blades of the scissors or knife and cut slowly, with care and attention.

CUTTING

MANIPULATING PAPER

Paper can be creased, crinkled, crushed, pleated, and curled. By using a variety of manipulating techniques you can alter the general appearance and surface quality of the paper. If the paper has been constantly creased and crinkled it may start to wear, a quality that could be used to your advantage to create a distressed feel.

TEARING

A torn edge can provide an interesting contrast to a background, and there are various techniques of tearing to choose from.

1 To tear a circle or part of a circle, hold a plate over the sheet of paper and tear the paper along the plate's curved edge.

2 Use a metal ruler to tear in a straight line. Place the ruler on the sheet of paper and tear the paper along the ruler's edge.

3 You can tear any shape freehand, and with practice you will become more accurate.

PASTING

In most cases you will apply glue to a collage piece and position it on the base sheet. However, at other times you may find it easier to apply the glue to the base sheet.

1 Use a paintbrush to brush the glue onto the back of a collage piece.

2 Turn the glued sheet over and position it on the base sheet. Use a clean, dry paintbrush to brush the piece into position, working from the middle toward the edges to expel any trapped air.

3 Continue pasting the remaining elements into place. If you have a brayer or similar small roller, work it over the whole collage to make sure all the pieces are stuck down.

THE COMPLETED TORN COLLAGE

The torn edges of the handmade paper used for this example provide interesting texture and contrast details.

COMPOSITION

THE COMPOSITION OF YOUR WORK—WHERE YOU PLACE EACH PAPER SHAPE AND PATTERN—IS CRUCIAL TO THE OVERALL EFFECT OF THE FINISHED PIECE. THE COLLAGE CAN BE REPRESENTATIONAL OR ABSTRACT, ELEMENTS CAN BE ARRANGED RANDOMLY OR SYMMETRICALLY, AND THE WHOLE PIECE CAN BE AS SIMPLE OR COMPLEX AS YOU LIKE.

SEE ALSO

Cutting and Pasting, pages 122–123

WORK IN PROGRESS

Take time over the planning stage to help you visualize the finished work in a rough format. You can use a sketchbook or pinboard to help you to collate your collage pieces and hone down your ideas. You may find it useful to arrange images according to color or subject matter, and will likely see a theme develop.

It is important to assess your work constantly as it progresses, and do not be afraid to discard elements that are not working. Reposition the elements as many times as necessary to achieve the desired effect: accidental discoveries made by arranging and rearranging pieces can be very exciting.

LINKS

Using collage pieces with similarities in shape, color, and tone can help to link disparate areas and create an integrated whole. Think about how the background will interact with the elements placed over it. Ask yourself whether large plain areas need to be broken up with smaller pieces, or whether detailed areas need to be separated by a contrasting color or flat shape.

BALANCE AND SCALE

Scale of shapes and pattern plays an important part in balancing a piece of work. If everything is of the same scale the picture may look static and lifeless. The addition of pattern or shape of a different scale will add movement and interest.

COLOR

Careful use of color can help to balance a design. It is wise not to have a picture made of only dark or light colors. For example, a dark collage will look overpowering, but can be lightened considerably if hints of a lighter color are added.

Having too much of one particular color may throw off the balance of the finished work. So, if one color appears as a large shape or fills a single area, use a little of it somewhere else in the work.

CREATING A BACKGROUND

The nature of the background imagery and the style of its creation depend on the theme and mood of the overall image.

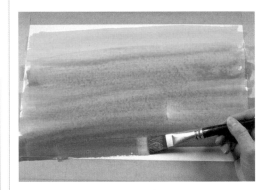

Using paint on commercial papers is an easy way to create your own surface. Watercolors give a subtle, watery background. For a graduated effect, choose three colors that blend well together. Paint one-third of the paper with the first color, then paint the next third with the next color, starting by overlapping the two colors. Repeat with the third color and use a damp brush to blend the seams between colors.

CEATHRAMH GARBH, ARDMORE, SUTHERLAND ANN DAVIDSON
The focal point of this collage is the small lake at the center of the hillocks. The artist tries out a number of combinations with colored torn paper, until just the right composition becomes apparent.

You could take as your starting point images of a similar color. Arrange a selection of images according to the tone of the color or by size or subject matter. Here the largest areas of blue are laid down first, then smaller parts are added to the basic square shape.

A background can also be built up in strips. Choose papers of similar colors or, as here, papers that feature similar textures, for a unified feel. Trim all the strips to the same width, then fix them together using glue on overlapping edges, or paste them to a backing of paper or card.

OVERLAYING

Once you have created a background, the focal-point details can be overlaid. Several layers can go on top of each other, with various parts of each visible from underneath the next. Or there may be only one extra layer on top of the background.

Experiment with the arrangement of your overlaid pieces, considering their size and shape and position on the background. The people, due to their size, make for good middle-ground detail in this beach scene.

Translucent layers can be overlaid to allow the background to show through. Photocopy your image onto tracing paper and layer it over your background to decide on the preferred position. Cut the shape out and use a dilute PVA glue mix to paste in place.

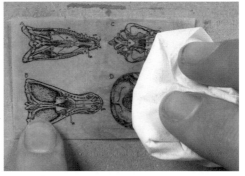

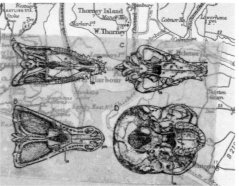

You can make paper semitransparent by applying a generous amount of linseed oil to your selected image using a paintbrush. Allow to soak in well, then remove excess oil with a cloth. Apply glue to the reverse side, place it over your background, and press down firmly. When the glue has dried parts of the background will be visible through the paper.

PROJECT

PAINTED PAPER COLLAGE

THIS COLLAGE PROJECT INTERPRETS AN ACTUAL STILL LIFE IN AN ACCURATE AND REALISTIC WAY.

Working directly with a subject matter in front of you will make your interpretation of the shapes and colors more accurate. Start by painting white paper with the required colors, or, if you prefer, use store-bought colored papers. Use a good-quality paper as a base for painting, so that the paper doesn't warp. Once the painted papers have dried they can be torn into the background, bowl, and fruit shapes.

SEE ALSO
Cutting and Pasting, pages 122–123
Composition, pages 124–125

WHAT YOU WILL NEED
- Good-quality papers
- Watercolor paints: Prussian blue, lemon yellow, purple madder, Naples yellow, white, and sap green
- 1 sheet of tissue paper
- Paintbrushes
- Metal ruler
- Pencil
- Pastels
- PVA glue

COLLAGE PIECES
Carefully choose which areas of the painted paper to tear into which shapes, allowing yourself to be guided by the color and texture of the paper. Add details with pastel or more watercolor as desired.

1 Begin by painting all of the papers. Paint flat washes of Prussian blue, lemon yellow, purple madder, and Naples yellow mixed with white. Don't worry about uneven marks in the washes, since these add to the charm of the finished collage. Allow the papers to dry.

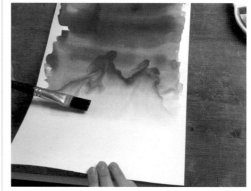

2 Paint a graduated wash of sap green, diluting the paint with a little more water as you work down the paper, to achieve the graduation. Areas from this will be used to create the light and dark tones of the pears. Paint one sheet of tissue paper with sap green, and leave both papers to dry.

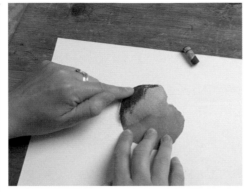

3 Tear the tissue paper along the grain with long, easy strokes, into strips ½in. (1.3cm) wide. To make a checked tablecloth, place strips in horizontal rows about 1in. (2.5cm) apart and fix into position with PVA glue. Fix vertical strips in the same way.

5 Add shading to the shapes by drawing and smudging pastel on the torn paper pieces. Use your finger to rub the pastel marks and blend them together for a soft effect.

6 Assemble the background, then the fruit, and finally the bowl. Keep adjusting and tearing the shapes as necessary. When you are happy with the arrangement, apply glue to the reverse side of each piece and fix in place.

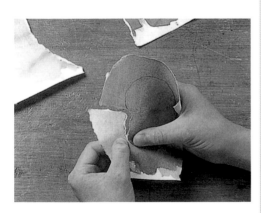

4 To make the individual shapes, tear the painted papers into manageable pieces. Sketch an outline of the shapes onto the papers and tear just inside the pencil lines using short, precise movements.

PAINTED PAPER COLLAGE
Layering and overlapping of all elements gives this collage picture a good sense of depth.

UNIT 9

PAPIER MÂCHÉ

IN RECENT YEARS, PAPIER MÂCHÉ HAS UNDERGONE A MAJOR REVIVAL. ITS VERSATILITY AND LOW-TECH METHOD MAKE IT THE IDEAL MEDIUM FOR THE CRAFTSPERSON WITH LITTLE SPACE OR FEW FACILITIES.

FINISHES

Various varnishes can be used to seal and protect a papier mâché piece, as well as imparting the desired finish, for example completely matte or with a soft sheen. Choose acrylic paints if you wish to color your piece.

GRETA (THE GUARDIAN CAT)
ANAT BAR AM

Cats are a symbol of luck in many cultures, and some believe that they watch over us. This sculpture recycles plastic bottles and creates art that will help clean the world and make people smile. The body of the sculpture is made from the upper part of a bottle, topped with rolled-up newspaper to shape a head. The decoration theme features delicate bright red flowers on a meadow background.

PARROTS
JOANNA JEDRZEJEWSKA

These papier-mâché parrots contain a "skeleton" made from wire, newspaper, and aluminum foil. They are brightly painted with acrylic paints over a layer of gesso, and the smooth finish is completed with several coats of acrylic varnish.

BRIEF HISTORY

Papier mâché is a French term meaning "mashed paper." It was first coined, not in France but in eighteenth-century London, by French émigré workers who made papier-mâché objects in small workshops. Only recently have the French themselves recognized the term.

PAPERS

Large-format newspapers are most often used, since their paper is of a better quality than tabloid newsprint, and it is much more flexible and adaptable when soaked with paste or glue. Using alternate layers of pink and white newspaper makes counting the layers easier. You can also layer with different kinds of paper. Fewer layers would be necessary if using thicker, handmade papers, although they would need to be torn into smaller pieces to cover a curved surface without creasing. Tissue paper will produce a delicate but fragile piece.

Colored or dyed paper can also be used, thus enhancing and revealing the technique of layering, while integrating the decoration of the piece with its construction. Experimenting with different kinds and strengths of paper is an exciting and worthwhile way to explore the many possibilities of this technique.

METHODS

Papier mâché is a laminating technique used to cast from a mold or former, and involves building up many layers of torn pasted paper. The paper is torn into strips—along the grain—rather than cut, because tearing produces smoother and less obvious joins when pasted down. When casting from a more complicated form it is better to use smaller, thinner pieces of newspaper. These will mold themselves to the form without creasing.

The number of layers laid down depends on the required thickness of the finished article. About ten would be enough for a bowl that will be further strengthened with paint or varnish. About eight layers would be sufficient for a mask. Lay the paper in one direction for one layer, then crosswise for the next, to give the piece more strength. Smooth each piece of paper down with the fingers so that no air or lumps of paste are trapped between the layers, since these will disfigure the final piece when dry. It is possible to add all the layers in one go, but allowing each layer to dry before applying the next produces a more reliable finish. This is a matter of personal preference however; each artist discovers and refines their own techniques.

Wallpaper paste and/or PVA glue are used for papier mâché. You can mix the two glues to the consistency of double cream. Spread the glue or paste onto each side of the strip of paper separately and allow it to soak through the paper to render it more flexible, although it should not be wet. It is a good idea to paste up a few pieces at a time and lay them around the edge of the paste bowl ready for use. They will soon dry, so use them quickly. Alternatively, paste up a large piece of paper before tearing into strips.

CREAMY BOWL
JOANNA JEDRZEJEWSKA
This bowl has been formed using an inflated balloon as a mold. Papier-mâché strips are applied to the mold, followed by a final layer of paper pulp (see pages 136–141). When everything is dry, the balloon is burst, and the bowl finished with paints and varnish.

HARE
NANCY WINN
This charming piece by Nancy Winn captures the shy yet inquisitive nature of the hare. Nancy works with recycled materials to create art that is fun and easy to understand. Much like clay, papier mâché is an expressive medium much suited to the creation of three-dimensional art.

CASTING FROM A FOUND MOLD

IT IS POSSIBLE TO MAKE ONE-PIECE CASTS USING A HUGE RANGE OF OBJECTS AS MOLDS, AS LONG AS THEIR SHAPES ARE NOT COMPLICATED.

CHOOSING MOLDS

Balloons, plates, bowls, flowerpots, and even woks make good molds. When choosing a suitable mold, consider whether you should cast from the inside rather than the outside, in order to release the paper cast in one piece, since there is a certain amount of shrinkage of the paper during the drying process.

CASTING A BOWL

A bowl is one of easiest molds to start with. To get a good finish, the layers need to be worked with care, so don't rush.

1 Cover the inside of a bowl with a releasing agent such as petroleum jelly or soft soap. Take care to include the inside and top of the rim. Tear the newspaper down the grain in strips 1½in. (4cm) wide. Tear again into lengths of 3in. (8cm).

2 Put the paste of your choice into a bowl: this can take the form of PVA glue, wallpaper paste, or a mix of the two. Apply the paste to the paper strips in small batches as you work. Paste each piece separately with the fingers, making sure the strips are not soaked and that there are no lumps of paste attached.

ETRUSCAN SPRING
RENÉE PARKER

The mold for this pitcher, inspired by the artist's love of ancient artifacts, has been built from salvaged materials. The rudimentary shape is made by taping a paper cone to the bottom of a small balloon, with a piece of cardboard tube at the top; the handle is formed from a piece of hanger wire. The unique shapes of the neck, spout, and handle are created by layering more strips of newspaper in some areas than in others. Once dry, the balloon is popped and pulled out, the papier-mâché surface is sanded until very smooth, and several layers of acrylic paint and matte sealant are applied to achieve a weathered look.

3 Lay pasted strips of paper in the mold, smoothing each piece separately and overlapping each one. Continue until the first layer is complete. You may prefer to allow the first layer to dry before applying the second, or move straight on with the next stage.

4 Lay a second layer of paper over the first, crosswise for strength, using paper of a different color for each layer if possible. Cover very evenly. Continue with alternating colors until ten layers are completed, remembering to smooth each layer to eliminate any bubbles. Leave to dry.

5 When the bowl is completely dry, ease the top of the cast away from the mold.

6 Twist the dry papier mâché and the cast bowl will release. If there is any reluctance, or if the first layer seems damp, leave to dry for a little longer.

7 Cut the rim evenly with a craft knife, and add two layers of pasted paper to cover the sharp cut edge.

DRYING METHODS

Drying times vary according to the working environment. It is always best to let the piece dry at an even temperature in a warm place—an airing cupboard is ideal. Drying may be speeded up by using an oven on a very low temperature. Rapid drying may cause distortion, and could cause the mold to degenerate, depending on what it is made from.

DECORATIVE DETAILS
In the case of a bowl, there are many alternative and imaginative ways to treat the rim, which will influence the bowl's form and character. For example, when layering, allow the torn paper to project from the mold and, when thoroughly dry, tear into a deckle edge. The rim may be cut unevenly, scalloped, or zigzagged, or be cut through like latticework. Here, six layers of pasted paper strips have been added to the rim, which is being cut to shape.

DRIP
RENÉE PARKER
A plastic bottle acts as a quick, inexpensive mold. Newspaper strips dipped in white glue are applied to the top, dome-shaped part of the bottle. Once dry, the dome is cut off the bottle and the seam taped back together. A "drip" shape cut from cereal box cardboard is taped to the narrowest end to make the bottom of the cup, and a handle shaped from salvaged wire is taped to the side. Paper strips are applied to the whole form and when dry the cup is sanded and painted with acrylic paint. The outside is sealed with a matte sealant, and the inside has several applications of a high-gloss sealant, to imitate glazed ceramics.

USING OTHER MOLDS

ANOTHER APPROACH TO THE LAYERING METHOD IS TO CONSTRUCT YOUR OWN MOLD. THIS ALTERNATIVE OFFERS NUMEROUS POSSIBILITIES. THE SIMPLEST, PERHAPS, IS A TRADITIONAL RELIEF MASK, BUT IT IS ENTIRELY POSSIBLE TO MAKE THREE-DIMENSIONAL OBJECTS, WHERE THE PAPER IS LAYERED ON ALL SIDES OF THE MOLD.

SEE ALSO
Casting From a Found Mold, pages 130–131
Decorative Ideas, pages 134–135

MATERIALS

The most useful material for creating your own mold is children's soft modeling clay, which can be molded into myriad shapes. Plaster of Paris can be used in conjunction with the modeling clay to create a more permanent mold that can be used again and again.

MAKING A MODELING CLAY MOLD

Children's soft modeling clay is one of the simplest and most convenient materials to use to make your own molds.

1 To make a relief mold, place a slab of rolled-out modeling clay on the work surface and use a knife or wooden modeling tool to cut out the outline. Carve pieces away from areas that require thinning.

2 Add on details formed from other pieces of modeling clay by overlapping them with the main form and smoothing the join with fingers or the modeling tool.

3 When you are satisfied with the shape of the mold, inscribe surface texture with various tools. Take care not to create any sharp undercuts or over-projecting details that will prevent the release of the cast.

4 To make a three-dimensional, freestanding mold, shape the clay in your hands and add extra elements and surface detail in the same way as for a relief mold.

TAMASHI BIRDS
ANAT BAR AM

Momma Luna and her chick Sunny are created from plastic bottles and newspaper. The pair express nature, hence the moon and the sun adorning their heads, and the decorations of clouds, hills with trees, flowers, and butterflies. Anat uses a pen to create the delicate drawings, and water-soluble aquarelle crayons to create various effects with color. To protect their delicate nature, the birds are covered with a layer of varnish.

MAKING A PLASTER MOLD

A more permanent mold for a mask or a relief form can be made from plaster of Paris.

CASTING FROM A HOMEMADE MOLD

When you are sculpting your mold from the initial modeling clay, take care not to allow any part to project too far, since this will cause difficulties when releasing the cast.

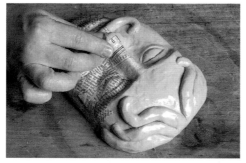

1 Model the form with modeling clay, then build a retaining wall with wooden battens or clay 1in. (2.5cm) higher than the mold. The whole structure should be built on a wooden board and the walls sealed to the board to prevent seepage. Mix the plaster according to the instructions, until it becomes creamy. Pour this mixture gently into the mold until it reaches the top of the retaining wall. Bang the work surface to force out any bubbles trapped inside.

1 Coat the mold with an even layer of petroleum jelly or soft soap. Prepare and paste paper strips as for casting from a found mold, but make the pieces much smaller to allow them to curve around the intricate shapes of the mold. Apply the first layer of paper, smoothing it to remove air bubbles and excess paste.

3 Trim the uneven edge of the mask, so that it can lie flat.

4 Cover the cut edges of the mask with two layers of paper. Allow to dry thoroughly before painting.

2 The plaster warms as it sets. When set, turn over and remove the clay. Allow the mold to dry thoroughly, then coat with shellac to seal the surface. The plaster mold is a negative, and can be used for layering papier mâché or for casting with pulp (see page 140–141).

2 Cover with eight layers of paper in alternate colors, and allow to dry thoroughly. Release the cast by prising the edges away from the clay with fingers or a blunt knife.

THE COMPLETED PAPIER-MÂCHÉ CAST

The completed cast can be painted with acrylic paint (see page 135).

DECORATIVE IDEAS

TECHNIQUES FOR DECORATING AND EMBELLISHING PAPIER MÂCHÉ OBJECTS ARE LIMITLESS. ILLUSTRATIONS OF FINE DECORATIVE FINISHES MAY PROVIDE INSPIRATION, BUT THERE ARE NO SET RULES, AND DECORATION IS UP TO YOUR OWN IMAGINATION.

Interesting decorative effects may be achieved by adding objects to form a relief pattern, either under the final layer of paper, or on top of it but under a primer layer of paint. String can provide free-flowing embossed lines, while seeds, shells, and pieces of cardboard may be glued in place.

SEALING

The papier-mâché surface needs priming before decorating. This will prevent the paint from being absorbed by the porous paper. Acrylic primer gives a good, matte white surface to work on.

FELIX
RENÉE PARKER
This piece is one of a series inspired by the artist's grandmother's teacup collection. Strips of newspaper are layered onto the top portion of a juice bottle, around the neck, to form the bowl of the cup. Once dry, the bowl shape is cut to release it from the bottle and the seam taped back together. A handle shaped from salvaged wire is added, and a circle cut from salvaged cardboard taped in place to form the bottom of the cup. After layering the whole piece with papier mâché, it is dried and sanded smooth, then painted with acrylic paint. Matte sealant is applied to complete the piece.

Before priming it is possible to go some way toward waterproofing a papier-mâché piece by coating it with three or four layers of linseed oil, before baking at a low temperature until completely dry.

VARNISHES

A variety of finishes can be achieved using different varnishes. Many layers of polyurethane varnish, sanded lightly between each coat, will produce a glassy effect. However, the varnish has the disadvantage of yellowing with age. A single coat of matte water-based varnish will seal a painted surface, but will not be obviously visible. Papier-mâché objects treated with varnish will never be completely waterproof, and must not be expected to hold liquids. They can, however, be wiped clean with a damp cloth without damage.

A more interesting surface can be obtained with the use of traditional lacquer. It dries hard, so strengthening the piece and giving it a finish that resembles porcelain. The lacquer itself may be colored with powder paint. An ancient-looking mottled effect can be created by painting color layer by layer over the lacquer, sanding each layer as it dries.

SEE ALSO
Casting From a Found Mold, pages 130–131
Using Other Molds, pages 132–133

TEXTURED PAINTING

Papier-mâché objects can be painted with brushes, sponges, or rags. Acrylic or gouache (water-based) paints are ideal.

HANDMADE PAPER AND GOLD LEAF

The application of precious-metal leaf is a surprisingly uncomplicated process that will magically transform papier mâché. Here it is combined with handmade papers that are used as the final layer of the papier mâché.

1 Paint on a coat of acrylic primer and leave to dry completely.

1 Tear spirals, squares, and circles from a variety of handmade papers. Paste all over the shapes and overlap them on the surface of the papier-mâché form. Allow to dry.

3 Gently press the gold-leaf shapes onto the glue and peel the paper backing away from the gold leaf.

2 For a bright, uniform effect, apply acrylic paint at its full intensity. To apply a subtle wash, dilute the paint first.

2 Cut some gold leaf into strips or other shapes. Brush PVA glue on the papier-mâché surface in the places where the gold leaf will be placed, and leave until it becomes tacky.

4 When dry, seal the decoration with water-based varnish.

3 You can add texture by applying a wash and removing some of the paint with a rag. Or dip a kitchen towel in paint and dab it onto the cast.

THE COMPLETED DECORATION
Neutral shades have been used to decorate this plate, but you could use differently colored pages as desired.

EQUIPMENT CHECKLIST

Most of the equipment used to make pulp can be found in the kitchen.

- Scissors
- Selection of mixing bowls
- Blender (food processor) or electric whisk
- Sieve
- Protective gloves
- Cardboard (this can be used to make a base onto which paper pulp can be layered)
- Craft knife (used to cut a cardboard base)
- Strong adhesive tape
- PVA glue
- Paintbrush
- Acrylic primer
- Mold
- Plastic wrap

UNIT 10

PAPER PULPING

AN ALTERNATIVE BUT SIMILAR TECHNIQUE TO LAMINATING PAPIER MÂCHÉ IS PAPER PULPING. INSTEAD OF USING TORN PAPER YOU CAN MAKE UP A PAPER PULP AND COMBINE IT WITH PASTE. THIS CAN THEN BE PRESSED INTO OR SHAPED OVER A MOLD OR FORMER, GLUED TO A BASE STRUCTURE, OR EVEN SHAPED WITHOUT A MOLD.

SHREDDED PAPER

Many people like the security of shredding their own documents at home. Go one step further and use the shredded documents to make paper pulp.

IN RIMA AI DUSCINETTI D'AUTUNNO
IRMA IRSARA

A flat light blue layer of pulp forms the basis of this piece. To create the airborne leaf shape in the middle, multiple layers of autumnal reds and oranges are laid down. Twisted paper twine is embedded into and pulled away from the leaf, leaving an impression, and reincorporated into the piece to create a three-dimensional effect.

RED BOOTS
ERIKA TAKACS

This piece is inspired by the seven-mile boots from a tale by the brothers Grimm. Erika covers a wire armature with a commercial paper pulp. After the hardening of the first layer, a second layer is added to the figure to replace lost detail due to shrinkage. It is finished with acrylic paint and sealed with a water-based sealer.

WHIMSICAL FISH LAMPS
BARBARA FLETCHER
Barabara Fletcher's unique method of working with paper pulp is to spray it in many overlapping layers onto wire screening, using an air gun designed for spraying ceilings with textured paint, but adapted for the bulkier pulp. The resulting sculpture is then painted with fabric dyes. Barbara discovered the illuminated beauty of the paper pulp texture after holding a sprayed piece over a light source.

PAPERS
This is a good way to recycle your shredded documents, alternatively tear strips from any paper that is neither glossy nor coated. Newspaper, photocopy paper, leaflets, and even junk mail can all be useful sources of the ideal raw ingredient.

METHODS
Adding wallpaper paste to a pulp made from recycled paper makes a modeling medium that sets hard and holds together well. Paper pulping is a much quicker method for building up thickness than papier-mâché layering, and objects made using pulp are less likely to warp. As well as casting using a mold, you can model paper pulp onto an existing base with the help of a little PVA glue. Making the pulp requires the use of kitchen equipment, including a blender (food processor) and sieve. If these items are going to be used regularly for paper pulping it is probably worth acquiring some just for this purpose. However, if they are going to be used only occasionally, provided they are washed thoroughly after use, they will not be damaged.

DECORATION
Objects made using paper pulp can be finished using any of the techniques detailed for papier mâché (see Decorative Ideas, page 134).

MAGIC PUMPKINS
LIAT BINYAMINI ARIEL
These pumpkins are made from recycled paper pulp, mixed with water and glue. The pulp is applied onto a pumpkin-shaped mold made from used plastic grocery bags. When the outside is completely dry the lid is cut open, and all of the plastic bags are taken out, allowing the inside of the pumpkin to dry. The pumpkin is then sanded, primed, painted, and varnished just like any other papier-mâché artwork.

PREPARING THE PULP

AS WITH PAPERMAKING, THE PULP IS MADE BY SOAKING AND PROCESSING SMALL PIECES OF PAPER. THE ADDITION OF WALLPAPER PASTE, HOWEVER, IS WHAT MAKES THIS A ROBUST AND LIGHTWEIGHT MEDIUM THAT IS SUITABLE FOR CASTING AND MODELING TO CREATE THREE-DIMENSIONAL OBJECTS.

**ESPERIENZE DI COLORE
IRMA IRSARA**
Inspired by light viewed through a waterfall, Irsara layers pulp of contrasting colors. Twisted paper twine is embedded in the pulp and stripped away to reveal the colors underneath. Some of the removed strips are then glued back elsewhere. Irsara dries her work slowly and naturally in the open air in order to achieve maximum strength and intensity of color.

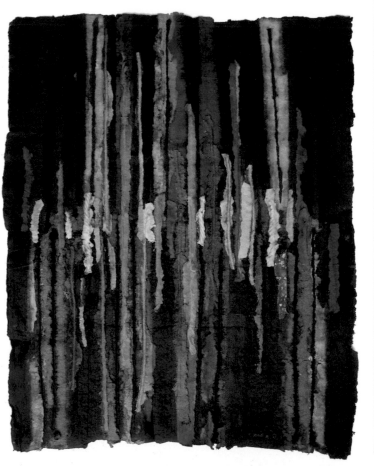

PREPARING THE PAPER

If you are using sheets of paper, tear them into squares of about 1½in. (4cm). Shredded paper should be cut to lengths of about 2in. (5cm), since longer strips will wrap around the shaft of the blender mechanism and strangle it.

MAKING PULP

1 Soak the paper pieces in a large bowl of water for at least three hours, although overnight is preferable. Place a small handful of soaked paper in a blender then top up with water to the maximum level indicated on the jug. Liquidize the mix until the paper is reduced to a pulp.

2 Pour the contents of the blender through a sieve to drain the water from the pulp. Agitate the pulp in the sieve to remove excess water. The pulp should be damp but not dripping.

3 Crumble the pulp to break it up into pieces. Repeat Steps 1 and 2 until you have enough pulp for your project.

COLORED PAPER

You can make a colored pulp simply by using colored papers. Construction paper, colored napkins, and tissue paper are good examples.

ARRESTARSI AI RAGGI NOTTURNI IRMA IRSARA
Dyed pulp is laid down in layers of color from light to dark, wet on wet. The greens and yellows evoke the feel of watercolors, and the artist did need to control the amount of water used in the pulps in order to monitor the bleed between colors. The colors chosen reflect dense forest, moss-covered trees, and glimpses of bright moonlight.

4 Mix wallpaper paste to a fairly thick consistency and, wearing protective gloves if preferred, gradually add paste to the pulp, until the pulp is pliable but not wet. When squeezed into a column 2in. (5cm) high it should remain upright. If it falls over it is too wet so add more pulp. If it is dry and crumbly add more paste.

APPLICATIONS

AS WITH PAPIER MÂCHÉ, PULP CAN BE CAST USING FOUND OBJECTS SUCH AS BOWLS AND PLATES, OR IT CAN BE MOLDED OVER A BASE.

SEE ALSO

Casting from a Found Mold, pages 130–131
Using Other Molds, pages 132–133
Decorative Ideas, pages 134–135

**EVOLUTION
ERIKA TAKACS**

Inspired by The Thinker and Seated Woman, two Neolithic figurines from the Hamangia culture, this sculpture reflects upon evolutionary processes triggered by gene mutation, natural selection, and interbreeding between Neanderthals and Homo Sapiens, long suspected, and now confirmed by the latest research studies. A steel screen armature is covered with a commercially bought paper pulp, and the sculpture is sealed with a water-based sealer and lightly patinated with acrylic paint.

An easy way to make large pieces is to start with a cardboard base, build up bulk with newspaper, then cover this base structure with a thin layer of paper pulp. By building in this way, less pulp is used and it dries faster and more evenly. Any type of cardboard can be used to make the base, including corrugated cardboard, mounting card, cartons, carpet rolls, and tubes. To make an especially strong base, laminate several layers of cardboard together with glue.

PULPING ONTO A CARDBOARD BASE
The cardboard structure—not the pulp—gives the piece its strength, so it is important to attach handles or other additions very firmly before the pulp is added.

1 Design the cardboard base and use a craft knife to cut out all the elements. Use strong tape to fix the elements together to make a solid structure—in this example a tray.

2 Use crumpled newspaper to build up the rim by gluing and taping it into place.

3 Brush PVA glue onto the base in stages, and mold the pulp firmly into place over it.

4 The pulp is strong enough to be molded freehand into small decorative motifs.

5 Continue applying glue and pulp to cover the whole base. Add more pulp to areas that need extra strengthening. Leave to dry thoroughly.

6 When the tray is completely dry, brush on a coat of acrylic primer to seal the surface.

THE COMPLETED TRAY
The tray can be finished using paints and varnishes.

CASTING A PLATE
Make sure the pulp is dry before you attempt to remove it from its mold.

1 To begin, line the top of the plate mold with plastic wrap.

2 Press the paper pulp evenly onto the inside of the plate mold to a thickness of about ¼–½in. (6mm–1.3cm). Leave to dry slightly.

3 Smooth the surface of the pulp with the back of a metal spoon.

4 Decorate the rim with more pulp, then leave to dry in a warm place.

5 Remove the pulp plate from the mold. Finish the underside by making a foot rim with more pulp. When the pulp is completely dry, seal the cast with a coat of acrylic primer.

USING OTHER MOLDS

You can buy craft molds suitable for making Christmas decorations or small casts to stick on cards or book covers. Alternatively, try using jelly or candy molds.

EQUIPMENT CHECKLIST

To make recycled paper or plant fiber pulp you will need the following:

- Protective tablecloths and aprons
- Scissors
- Blender (food processor)
- Glass jars
- Sieve
- Papermaking pigments (if you wish to color your pulp, then these give the best results)
- Fireplace ashes (these make a good alkaline solution when breaking down plant fibers)
- Saucepans (only necessary when preparing plant fibers)
- Protective gloves (wear these when preparing alkaline solutions for plant material preparation)
- Size

To form sheets of paper you will need:

- Mold and deckle
- Vat
- Two boards, larger all around than your couching pad (these should be rigid and nonabsorbent; if wood is used, prime it first)
- Blankets
- Felts
- 4 G-clamps or several bricks
- Clothesline and clothespins, or a smooth surface such as glass, melamine, or linoleum
- Iron
- Paintbrush
- Knife
- Turkey baster and cookie cutters (optional)

UNIT 11

PAPER-MAKING

MOLD AND DECKLE

The purpose of the mold is to strain out water, leaving the fiber on the mesh to form the sheet of paper. The deckle gives shape to the sheet of paper while allowing for the natural "deckle edge" to form on every side, which is a distinctive feature of handmade paper.

MAKING YOUR OWN PAPER IS HIGHLY SATISFYING. A LITTLE TIME MUST BE SPENT BEFOREHAND TO PREPARE THE MOLD AND DECKLE AND TO GATHER EQUIPMENT, BUT ONCE EVERYTHING IS ASSEMBLED, PAPER CAN BE MADE TIME AND AGAIN.

PLANT PULPS AND NATURAL INCLUSIONS

Plants and flowers from the garden or the wild can be used to make the actual paper pulp, or may be embedded in the final sheet. Seeds, petals, leaves, and even whole flower heads give handmade papers a truly personal touch.

BRIEF HISTORY

For most of its 2,000-year history, paper has been made by hand. Only since the Industrial Revolution has the process become mechanized. The technology of modern papermaking is very complex, yet the basic process remains so simple that even a child can make paper.

PAPERS

Recycled papers can be used to make new sheets, including photocopy paper, advertisements, tissue paper, paper towels, and wrapping paper. However, avoid using paper that has a lot of black type on it: the plainer the better. Newspaper, being highly acidic, will turn yellow and brittle too quickly. Glossy magazines are also best avoided.

Plant fibers require a little extra preparation before being blended into a pulp. Some plants will only require cooking, while others will need the help of an alkaline solution to break down the fibers. A standard alkaline solution made from fireplace ashes, soda ash, or washing soda is adequate to treat most plant material. For tougher specimens, such as yucca or raffia, caustic soda is a stronger alternative. Wear protective gloves when making and using alkaline solutions.

SPECIAL EQUIPMENT

A mold and deckle is the piece of equipment used to actually form a sheet of paper. The mold is simply a frame with mesh stretched over it to catch the pulp and allow the water to drain through. The deckle is a frame, not unlike the mold, but completely open with no mesh stretched across it. During papermaking the deckle rests on top of the mesh side of the mold to confine the pulp to the size of the screened area, giving definition to the sheet of paper.

Mold and deckle sets are available through papermaking suppliers and through auctions of secondhand equipment. Alternatively, pieces of wire screening or fabric mesh can be stretched over a picture frame to make a mold. An identical frame without the screening may be used as the deckle.

A vat is a container for holding the mixture of water and pulp that you form the sheets from. It must be able to accommodate the mold and deckle in the act of sheet formation. A regular kitchen basin is a good size for a 5½ x 8½in. (14 x 21cm) mold and deckle set.

Felts are the pieces of fabric that each sheet of paper is "couched" or laid onto. The felt helps to hold the edge of the newly formed sheet as it is rolled off the mold. It also helps to absorb the water from the new sheet so that the fibers of pulp can lock together to form a strong bond. Nonwoven dishcloths are an inexpensive material to use, or try medium-weight sew-in interfacing—available from the dressmaking department of large stores—cut to size a little larger then your mold.

To create the couching pad and make the process of releasing the sheet from the mold that bit easier, a number of pieces of cut-up blanket may be placed under the first felt, and again over the final felt to protect the sheets when pressing out the excess water.

NOTECARDS
KATHY SAWATZKY
Recycled pulp with tiny dried yellow flowers combine to make this eye-catching stationery paper.

MOLDED BOWL
HEIDI REIMER-EPP
Formed from paper embedded with petals, and embellished with raffia and gold wire, this little bowl is a whimsical example of handmade paper art.

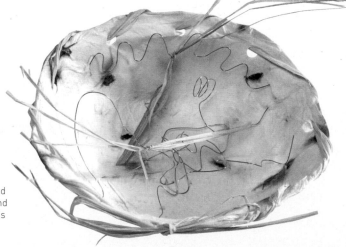

MAKING PULP

CAREFUL PREPARATION OF PULP WILL HELP ENSURE THAT YOUR PAPERMAKING EXPERIENCE IS SUCCESSFUL. ALWAYS WORK WITH SMALL AMOUNTS IN THE BLENDER, AND BLEND THOROUGHLY TO AVOID CLUMPS AND SPECKS IN YOUR PAPER.

STORING PULP

Unused pulp can be strained of water and stored in a refrigerator. Alternatively, squeeze out any excess water from the pulp and store balls of it in a freezer, or dehydrate them by air-drying and store in a dry place. A preservative (oil of cloves or thymol) can be added to give it a slightly longer life. Reused pulp may be of a slightly lower quality than newly prepared pulp, however it can be blended with new pulp. Never pour pulp mixture down the kitchen sink, since it will cause a blockage.

JOURNAL

As you experiment with using different paper- and plant fibers, and pigmenting the pulp, you may want to keep a papermaking journal in which you can list the ingredients used for each type of paper you make. Then when you come up with a sheet that you want to duplicate, you can reproduce the same great results.

SEE ALSO

Paper Grain, pages 10–11
Creasing and Cutting, pages 12–13

RECYCLED PAPER PULP

Paper pieces are soaked in water, and blended with water in batches.

1 Cut or tear the paper into squares of 1–2in. (2.5–5cm). Soak them in a bowl of water for at least 30 minutes, overnight. This begins the process of breaking down the fibers and making the pulp easier to beat in the blender.

2 Fill the blender three-quarters full with warm water, then add five or six pieces of the soaked paper. Secure the lid. Blend in short bursts, checking frequently to make sure the pulp has not collected around the blade.

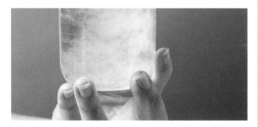

3 When there are no obvious lumps in the blended pulp, drop a pinch of it into a jar of water. Screw the lid on and shake the jar vigorously for one minute. Hold the jar up to the light to check for even consistency. If clumps of fiber are visible, more blending is required.

4 Pour the contents of the blender into the vat and continue pulping and filling. The vat needs to be three-quarters full to form sheets, however the pulp needs to be similar in texture to pancake batter, so if it is too heavy simply add water to the vat and mix thoroughly. With practice you can experiment with the texture in the vat to produce different thicknesses.

5 If you do not wish to use the pulp straightaway, or if you would like to color it with papermaking pigment, strain the pulp by pouring the contents of the blender through a sieve.

SIZING

If your finished paper sheets are to be used for painting, calligraphy, or printing, add size to the pulp to give a water resistance to the paper. The amount of size used will vary according to the purpose of the paper—writing paper needs to be more heavily sized than watercolor paper, for example. Always dilute the size in water before adding it to the pulp. Mix it in thoroughly and, for best results, allow the pulp to rest overnight before using.

PULP PIGMENTATION

The simplest way to make colored pulp is to use colored paper. Alternatively, the pulp can be pigmented using papermaking pigments, which are color- and lightfast.

PLANT-FIBER PULP

Before blending it into pulp, plant material needs to be broken down to separate the fibers and remove unwanted components. Nonfibrous material, for example carrot tops, can simply be simmered in a pan of water for one to two hours, until the toughest pieces pull apart easily. More fibrous material, however, requires the addition of an alkaline solution to help the process.

1 Add a small amount of pigment to a jar of water and stir well for about five minutes. This will make the distribution of the pigment within the pulp fibers more even.

1 Fibrous iris leaves can be broken down using a solution of fireplace ashes. Scrape both sides of the iris leaves with the tines of a fork to help in the breaking-down process.

4 Pour the liquid solution over the plant material and water to cover. Bring to a boil and simmer until the plant material is mushy and pulls apart easily. Strain and rinse the fibers several times to remove the alkaline solution.

2 Place strained pulp in the blender and slowly add the diluted pigment. Mix the pulp and pigment well on a low speed. For best absorption, leave the pigmented pulp overnight before using.

2 Cut the leaves into pieces about 1–2in. (2.5–5cm) long and soak these overnight in a saucepan of water to begin the process of breaking down the material.

5 Add a handful of processed plant material to a blender two-thirds full of water. Blend for a few seconds if a coarse paper is desired, or for longer if a smoother paper is required.

3 Then blend it once more before adding it to the vat.

3 Half-fill a saucepan with fireplace ashes and cover with water. Bring to a boil, stirring to dissolve the ash. Strain, discarding any undissolved product and save the liquid solution.

6 Add the pulp to the vat and top with water. Continue pulping and adding water until the vat is three-quarters full and the mix has the consistency of pancake batter.

MAKING THE PAPER

ONCE THE PULP IS IN THE VAT, A COUCHING PAD HAS BEEN PREPARED, AND THE MOLD AND DECKLE ARE AT THE READY, YOU CAN BEGIN TO PULL SHEETS OF PAPER.

The first sheet is often the most difficult to make. It may stick to the mold, or be too thick or too thin, or full of holes. With each piece you pull it will become easier, so do not worry when things go wrong.

COUCHING

The process of transferring the newly formed sheet onto another surface is called "couching." The term comes from the French verb *coucher* meaning "to lay down," a precise description of this technique, which allows multiple sheet forming with a single mold. The sheets are stacked in a "post" that can be up to 30 sheets high. You may find when couching that the pulp refuses to come off the mold. This could be because the sheet is too thin, in which case you need to put more pulp in the vat. Alternatively, the sheet might be too dry. Gently wet it again by placing the mold flat, pulp side up, just touching the surface of the water in the vat. This allows the pulp to soak up more water. Then try couching again.

SEE ALSO
Making Pulp, pages 144–145

THE COUCHING PAD

Before you pull the mold and deckle through the mix in the vat, prepare the couching pad that the sheet will be laid onto.

1 Fold a piece of blanket on a waterproof board. This makes it easier to roll the mold and deckle onto the couching surface, establishing connection between the pulp sheet and the surface of the couching pad.

2 Cover the pad with an unfolded piece of blanket to provide an absorbent layer.

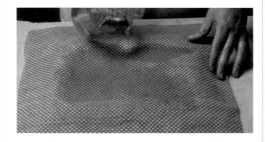

3 Lay a felt on top and smooth out any wrinkles, since these could transfer to paper. Pour water over the entire couching pad to increase the connection between the sheet and the couching surface. The pad should be damp rather than soaking wet.

PULLING A SHEET

Agitate the vat before pulling each sheet, to mix the pulp and water and ensure the pulp does not settle at the bottom. Try to develop the following steps into a smooth, continuous action.

1 Hold the deckle on top of the mold with thumbs on top. Reach toward the back of the vat and, in one continuous motion, pull the mold and deckle under the surface and up again.

2 As you begin to pull upward, hold the mold and deckle level with the surface of the water. This will make the pulp disperse evenly on the screen. Tipping the mold will cause thick deposits of pulp in some places and, as a result, a poor-quality sheet of paper.

3 Lift the mold and deckle straight up and out of the vat, breaking the surface tension and allowing some of the water to drain. Carefully remove the deckle from the mold to avoid dropping excess water onto the freshly formed sheet.

VATMAN'S TEARS

If water drips onto the sheet as you remove the deckle—a flaw known as vatman's tears—the sheet must be returned to the vat.

Hold the mold over the vat with the pulp facing downward. With a quick, firm motion, touch the mold's face to the surface of the water in the vat. The pulp lifts off and can be mixed back into the vat's pulp and reused.

COUCHING

To transfer the pulp on the mold to the couching pad you need to exert some pressure during the couching action. As with pulling sheets, you should aim to develop the following steps into a continuous motion.

1 Rest the longest edge of the mold on the cloth edge nearest you.

2 Roll the mold onto the cloth until it lies flat on the couching pad.

3 Press down firmly on the edges of the mold to make contact with the cloth.

4 Continuing the rolling motion, lift the bottom edge, and roll the mold off the pad, leaving the newly formed sheet behind on the couching pad.

5 Cover the sheet with two felts and repeat the pulling and couching processes. Cover with two more felts and continue until you form a stack of newly formed paper sheets separated by felts.

6 Cover the stack or post with a piece of blanket and place a waterproof board on top of the stack in preparation for pressing.

PRESSING AND DRYING

THE SHEETS YOU HAVE JUST FORMED CONSIST OF ABOUT 96 PERCENT WATER, SOME OF WHICH NEEDS TO BE REMOVED QUICKLY TO ALLOW THE SHEET TO BEGIN TO DRY.

PRESSING

The best way to remove excess water is to construct a press that will squeeze the water out while maintaining firm, even pressure that allows the pulp fibers to bond and make a strong piece of paper. Make sure you are prepared for the gush of water that will initially spill out of the press. After pressing, the damp sheets should be strong enough to pick up and transfer to their drying positions.

DRYING

Each papermaker will develop drying methods that best suit the particular surroundings, available materials, and varying conditions of their location. Temperature, humidity, space, and time are all contributing factors.

SEE ALSO

Making the Paper, pages 146–147

MAKING A PRESS

One way to squeeze out the water would be to stand on the top board and move gently around to press all areas. Alternatively you can use G-clamps or bricks to apply the necessary pressure.

1 Attach four G-clamps evenly around the boards at top and bottom of the post of papers. Tighten each clamp until water stops pouring from the stack.

2 If G-clamps are unavailable, use something heavy, such as a pile of bricks, to apply weight to the stack.

DRYING METHODS

Whether hung up or left to dry flat, where you dry your sheets will determine how quickly they will dry. The warmer the environment the better, which could mean in a heated indoor location or outside on a sunny day. Sheets left next to a radiator will dry quickly, although they may buckle.

2 To dry a sheet on a smooth surface, remove the sheet from the couching pad by holding its felt backing. Lay the felt with the sheet face down on the surface and carefully brush with a dry paintbrush. Then remove the felt. Leave to dry in a warm environment for about a week.

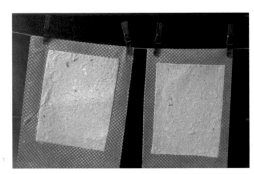

1 To hang sheets out to dry, remove the sheet from the couching pad by holding its felt backing. Fold over one edge of the felt and secure the overlapped edge to a clothesline using two clothespins. When dry, carefully peel the paper sheet from the felt. Press with a warm iron to flatten completely.

3 When the sheet is dry, use a knife to loosen the edges and carefully peel the sheet off the glass. The side against the surface will be smooth and glossy, while the air-dried surface will be rougher.

DECORATIVE TECHNIQUES

WITH THE BASIC TECHNIQUES MASTERED, YOUR PAPERMAKING CAN PROGRESS TO NEW LEVELS OF ARTISTIC CREATIVITY. EXPERIMENTING WITH DECORATIVE PAPERMAKING TECHNIQUES ALLOWS YOU TO CREATE PAPERS THAT ARE PERSONAL TO YOUR STYLE OR CUSTOMIZED FOR PARTICULAR USES.

SEE ALSO
....
Making Pulp, pages 144–145
Making the Paper, pages 146–147
Pressing and Drying, page 148

EMBEDDING TECHNIQUES: LAMINATING

Laminating is the process of couching two or more sheets on top of each other, which then bond together during pressing and drying to form a single, solid sheet of paper. The skill lies in lining up the top sheet so that it is placed exactly where you want it to be, whether directly on top of the base sheet, or at angles, or randomly applied.

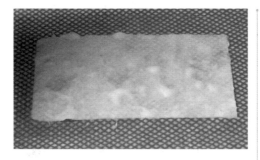

1 Pull and couch a sheet of paper in the usual way.

4 Pull and couch a second sheet directly on top of the first, using the threads as guidelines.

2 To ensure you align the second sheet precisely on top of the first, lightly position the deckle on the sheet and mark the outside edges with string or thread.

5 Carefully lift the mold and deckle away and press the sheet in a single layer to avoid embossing the motif onto other sheets of paper.

THE LAMINATED SHEET

The fibers of the pulp have merged together and the feather is encapsulated within a single sheet of paper.

3 Remove the deckle and position a feather, flowers, leaves, or any other small object that you wish to laminate on top of the sheet.

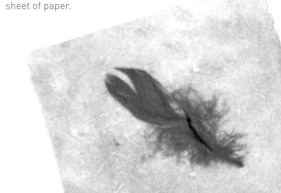

EMBEDDING TECHNIQUES: INCLUSIONS

Seeds, dried flowers, sequins, confetti, tea leaves, threads, and other small additions—even scented oils that can be smelt but not seen—can be added to the vat prior to pulling a sheet.

THE COMPLETED EMBEDDED SHEET
The scope for experimentation with this technique is vast, since multitude combinations of interesting and diverse inclusions can be tried.

2 Carefully lift up each object, using a knife if necessary to avoid marking the sheet with fingerprints. Hang the sheet up to dry.

1 Empty the inclusions into the vat and stir well to ensure they are evenly distributed.

EMBOSSING TECHNIQUES

It is possible to use embossing techniques with plant-fiber papers, however the most satisfactory results are achieved using recycled paper. The technique requires a thick sheet of paper, so increase the ratio of pulp to water in the vat.

1 Pull, couch, and lightly press a thick sheet of paper. Lay objects with transferable textures on the sheet and press each one down onto the paper as hard as possible.

3 To emboss using a press, position the embossing objects and cover the sheet with several felts and a few pieces of blanket. Press as usual but try not to apply too much pressure, since the embossing objects could go right through the paper. Remove the objects before hanging the sheet up to dry.

2 Pull a sheet and give the mold and deckle a strong shake from side to side to disperse the inclusions across the surface of the sheet. Couch and press, and dry on a smooth surface.

THE COMPLETED EMBOSSED SHEETS
Found objects such as keys, shoe prints, lace or woven fabrics, or anything with an interesting texture can make an impression on your handmade paper. Electrical wire is a useful material since it can be bent into any shape.

PAINTING WITH PULP

Applying pulp with a turkey baster takes practice. You do not want to squeeze the pulp out too quickly since it may blow away the pulp you have already applied, or part of the sheet on the mold. You may like to try out the technique on a sheet of dry scrap paper first.

The colored pulp also needs to be quite dilute so that it can be sucked up into the baster without getting stuck. Test the concentration of pulp with the baster and add water to the vat as necessary until you hit on the correct ratio.

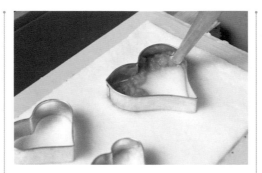

2 Draw a dyed, diluted pulp into the turkey baster. Position the baster over a cutter and gently squeeze to allow the pulp to come out. Move the baster around the outside of the shape as you squeeze, then fill in the center. Repeat with the other cutters and colors of pulp.

3 Carefully lift the cutters away from the mold and couch the sheet. You will see the underside of the sheet with the colored shapes showing through. Lightly press and dry on a smooth surface.

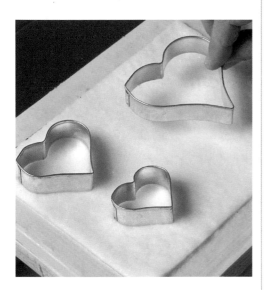

1 Place a mold with a pulled sheet over a shallow tray to catch excess water. Position cookie cutters or similar on the sheet, taking care not to press them down too firmly; they should just rest on the surface.

THE COMPLETED PULP-PAINTED SHEET
This technique gives an attractive, delicate effect.

PAPERMAKING RECIPES

WHILE EXPERIMENTING WITH PAPERMAKING IS AN EXCITING AND CREATIVE PROCESS, A LITTLE BACKGROUND KNOWLEDGE OF CERTAIN TECHNIQUES AND COMBINATIONS THAT HAVE PROVED SUCCESSFUL IN THE PAST CAN ONLY BENEFIT THE NOVICE PAPERMAKER.

RECIPES AND TECHNIQUES

Following on from the techniques of papermaking discussed so far, the recipes and decorative techniques featured over the next few pages have been tried and tested, and illustrate the results you can expect to achieve if you follow the instructions given. These examples provide an essential base of papermaking experience from which you can develop your own ideas and move forward. Remember that these recipes should be used in conjunction with the techniques for making pulps, making the paper, and drying sheets as detailed on pages 144–151.

SEE ALSO

Making Pulp, pages 144–145
Making the Paper, pages 146–147
Pressing and Drying, page 148
Decorative Techniques, pages 149–151

RECYCLED PAPER SAMPLERS

Different processing times on recycled paper pulp produce varying results in the end paper. The longer the pulp is blended, the smoother the final paper sheets will be, and if you are using printed paper, as here, the print will be visible in varying degrees. Experiment with your blender to produce the paper texture of your choice.

SMOOTH RECYCLED PAPER (A)

• *Recycled paper*
• *Water*

1 Soak the paper in water and process in the blender for 20 to 30 seconds, using short bursts of power.

2 Rinse the pulp and form sheets as usual. The paper will be smooth with very light traces of ink.

MEDIUM RECYCLED PAPER (B)

• *Recycled paper*
• *Water*

1 Soak the paper in water and process in the blender for 15 seconds, using short bursts of power.

2 Rinse the pulp and form sheets as usual. The paper will be smooth with some visible letters.

LIGHTLY CHUNKY RECYCLED PAPER (C)

• *Recycled paper*
• *Water*

1 Soak the paper in water and process in the blender for ten seconds, using short bursts of power.

2 Rinse the pulp and form sheets as usual. The paper will be more coarse and will feature some visible pieces of text.

HEAVILY CHUNKY RECYCLED PAPER (D)

• *Recycled paper*
• *Water*

1 Soak the paper in water and process in the blender for five seconds.

2 Rinse the pulp and form sheets as usual. The paper will be very coarse with large portions of visible text.

PAPER FROM HOME

Sources of recyclable paper are plentiful around the home. However, avoid using pages loaded with print, shredded paper, and Post-it notes, and look out for staples.

PIGMENTING PAPER

Construction papers are loaded with pigment and just a few pieces will effectively color a batch of recycled paper pulp. Adjust the blending times to determine the distribution of color: long blending will produce a smooth, even product, while short bursts will result in chunky pieces and separate color within the base pulp.

Tissue paper responds much like construction paper, except that it breaks down more easily, therefore does not require presoaking to break down the fibers, only to extract the dye.

COOL BLUE PAPER

- *4 torn sheets blue construction paper, approximately 1 x 1-in. (2.5 x 2.5-cm) pieces*
- *2 cups (500ml) water*
- *1 cup recycled paper pulp*

1 Soak the construction paper in the water for 10 to 15 minutes.

2 Add the soaked paper to the blender containing the recycled paper pulp. Blend the mixture for two to five seconds to achieve a medium-flecked pulp. If a more even shade is preferred, blend in longer bursts.

3 Form sheets as usual.

GREETINGS CARDS

- *1 cup torn greetings cards, approximately 3 x 3-in. (8 x 8-cm) pieces*
- *2 cups (500ml) water*

1 Select cards of different colors to add interest and contrast to the pulp. Soak the torn cards in the water for 30 minutes, longer if the paper is heavily coated.

2 Blend half of the paper for 30 to 60 seconds, or longer to create smooth pulp.

3 Add the remaining paper and lightly blend to produce chunks of color.

4 Rinse the pulp and form sheets as usual.

BROWN PAPER BAGS

- *1 cup torn brown paper bags, approximately 3 x 3-in. (8 x 8-cm) pieces*
- *2 cups (500ml) water*

1 Soak the torn paper in the water for 15 to 20 minutes.

2 Place several pieces in the blender and process for 30 seconds.

3 Continue to blend, adding the remaining paper until the mixture is smooth and creamy. Makes a lovely, light brown pulp.

4 Rinse the pulp and form sheets as usual.

PROPORTIONAL MEASURING

While the metric equivalent of a cup is 250ml, when referring to pulp the number of cups used in each recipe has not been converted. To ensure consistency, the papermaker is advised to use the same size vessel during the papermaking process, since proportion is more relevant than weight or volume.

CHERRY-FLECKED PAPER

- *2 torn sheets red construction paper, approximately 1 x 1-in. (2.5 x 2.5-cm) pieces*
- *1 torn sheet blue construction paper, approximately 1 x 1-in. (2.5 x 2.5-cm) pieces*
- *2 cups (500ml) water*
- *1 cup recycled paper pulp*

1 Soak the construction paper in the water for 15 minutes.

2 Place the soaked paper in the blender containing the recycled paper pulp. Lightly blend for five seconds. Make sure all the construction paper is pulped, but it should retain a chunky consistency.

3 Form sheets as usual.

PINK PIZAZZ

- *1 cup shredded fuchsia tissue paper*
- *1 cup (250ml) water*
- *½ cup recycled paper pulp*

1 Soak the tissue paper in the water for ten minutes.

2 Place the soaked paper and remaining water in the blender with the recycled paper pulp. Process well for five to ten seconds to achieve a smooth deep pink pulp.

3 Form sheets as usual.

EMBEDDING: LAMINATING

By arranging decorative items on a freshly couched sheet before laminating with a second sheet you can create interesting patterns in your paper.

CURLS

- *1 cup recycled paper pulp*
- *Embroidery thread, cut to different lengths*

1 Couch a base sheet of pink recycled paper pulp.

2 Arrange tiny curls of embroidery thread all across the sheet in a design of your choice. Couch a second, thin sheet of paper on top of the first.

3 Press and dry the sheet. The finished sheet will be delicately patterned.

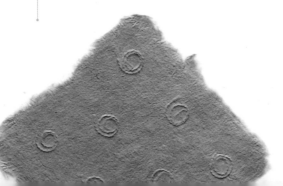

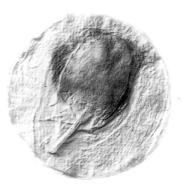

RAISED FLOWER

- *1 cup recycled paper pulp*
- *Chunky flower head*

1 Couch a base sheet of recycled paper pulp.

2 Place the flower head on the surface of the sheet. Couch another sheet of paper on top of the first.

3 To keep the three-dimensional look, do not press or weigh the sheet down, simply leave it to air dry.

FERN SURPRISE

- *1 cup recycled paper pulp*
- *Fern fronds*

1 Couch a base sheet of recycled paper pulp.

2 Position the fern fronds on the surface of the sheet. Couch another sheet of paper on top of the first.

3 Press and dry. Held up to the light, this sheet reveals the treasures within.

EMBEDDING: INCLUSIONS

Handmade papers with a sprinkling of colorful petals or other attractive natural materials are sought after and treasured. You can achieve countless variations by mixing assorted materials, following themes such as color, shape, size, or plant family.

CINNAMON AND RAFFIA

- *1 cup recycled paper pulp*
- *2 teaspoons (10ml) cinnamon powder*
- *½ cup raffia, cut into long, thin pieces*

1 Add the recycled paper pulp to the vat, adding water as necessary.

2 Mix the cinnamon and raffia strips with the pulp in the vat using a wire whisk.

3 Form sheets as usual. Produces a warm brown sheet with raffia accents.

DEEP PETAL BLEND

- *1 cup recycled paper pulp*
- *½ cup mix of deep red carnation petals and purple petals*

1 Add the recycled paper pulp to the vat, adding water as necessary.

2 Mix the petals together. Pour the petals into the vat and blend into the pulp with a wire whisk, ensuring an even distribution of material.

3 Form sheets as usual. Any deeply pigmented petals are likely to bleed into the pulp.

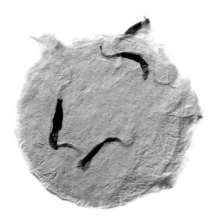

DRIED GERBERA DAISY

- *1 cup recycled paper pulp*
- *⅛ cup dried gerbera daisy petals*

1 Add the recycled paper pulp to the vat, adding water as necessary.

2 Evenly mix the dried petals into the pulp using a wire whisk.

3 Form sheets as usual. Dried gerbera daisy petals take on a deep, intense color. Here, the original deep orange has dried to a dark rust color.

EMBOSSING

Embossing using everyday objects from around the home allows you to give your handmade paper a variety of different textures. These textured sheets may be used for wall-hangings, as book covers (see page 80), or as artist's paper.

PAPER CLIP-EMBOSSED MOTIF

- *1 cup recycled paper pulp*
- *Large paper clip*

1 Couch a sheet of fresh paper.

2 Bend the paper clip to the desired shape and gently press it into the damp sheet.

3 Protect the sheet as necessary and weigh it down. Leave to air dry for 24 hours.

4 Remove the weight and make sure the sheet is completely dry before carefully removing the paper clip.

LEAF-EMBOSSED SHEET

- *1 cup recycled paper pulp*
- *Intact leaves*

1 Couch a sheet of fresh paper.

2 Gently press the leaves into the damp sheet in your chosen positions.

3 Protect the sheet as necessary and weigh it down. Leave for 24 hours to air dry.

4 Remove the weight and ensure the sheet is completely dry before carefully removing the leaves.

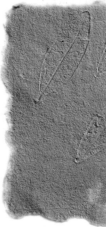

EMBOSSED WITH A NONCOLORFAST RUG
- *1 cup recycled paper pulp*
- *Woven rug*

1 Couch a fresh sheet of paper directly onto the rug.

2 Protect the paper as necessary and leave to air dry until damp.

3 While the paper is still a little damp, gently peel it away from the rug. Dye is likely to bleed into the paper, which can be very effective.

EMBOSSED WITH BUBBLE WRAP
- *1 cup recycled paper pulp*
- *Sheet of bubble wrap*

1 Couch a fresh sheet of paper directly onto the bubble wrap.

2 Do not weigh down the paper sheet, since this will burst the bubbles. Simply leave for 24 hours to air dry.

3 Carefully peel the dry sheet of paper away from the bubble wrap to reveal the honeycomb effect.

BRICK-EMBOSSED SHEET
- *1 cup recycled paper pulp*
- *House bricks*

1 Couch a fresh sheet of paper directly onto the bricks.

2 Protect the paper as necessary before applying a weight and leaving for 24 hours to air dry.

3 Gently peel the dry sheet away from the bricks and flatten the pattern edges with a warm iron.

WIRE-HEART EMBOSSED MOTIF
- *1 cup pulp*
- *Medium-gauge craft wire*

1 Bend a piece of medium-gauge craft wire into the desired shape, here a heart.

2 Couch the sheet of paper onto the shape.

3 Protect the sheet as necessary and weigh it down. Air dry.

4 When completely dry, peel the wire off the paper, leaving the heart shape visible.

PAINTING WITH PULP

Using this technique you can "paint" pictures—representational or abstract—with pulp. Remember to dilute the pulps you are "painting" with to give you more control over their use.

BLUE HEART
- *1 cup undyed recycled paper pulp*
- *½ cup blue recycled paper pulp*
- *Heart-shaped cookie cutter*

1 Pull a fresh sheet of undyed paper and leave on the mold, over a shallow tray.

2 Dilute the blue pulp until it is the consistency of cake mix batter.

3 Place the cookie cutter on the pulled sheet and pour the blue pulp into it.

4 Carefully lift the cutter away from the sheet and couch as usual. Protect and weigh down the sheet and leave to air dry completely.

PLANT PULPS

You can use almost any ordinary plant to make great paper. The nonfibrous materials can be cooked without an alkaline solution, but the fibrous leaves will require cooking with fireplace ashes, as described on page 147.

A

B

C

SCENE WITH FERNS

• *1 cup undyed recycled paper pulp*
• *⅓ cup blue recycled paper pulp*
• *Fern fronds*

1 Pull a fresh sheet of undyed paper and leave on the mold, over a shallow tray.

2 Dilute the colored pulps and beat well until each is the consistency of cake mix batter.

3 Using a spoon, or brush for more detail, apply the colored pulps randomly to the sheet. Position a few fern fronds and cover in places with more pulp.

4 When you are happy with the design, carefully couch the sheet as usual. Protect and weigh down the sheet and leave to air dry completely.

PURE CARROT TOPS (A)

• *1 cup carrot tops*
• *Water*

1 Cook the carrot tops in water for one to two hours. Drain and rinse.

2 Transfer the cooked tops to the blender and process for five seconds.

3 Rinse the pulp and form sheets as usual. Makes lovely dark green sheets.

CARROT TOPS AND RECYLED PAPER (B)

• *1 cup recycled paper pulp*
• *¼ cup cooked carrot tops (see*
• *Pure Carrot Tops)*

1 Process the paper pulp and cooked carrot tops in the blender until well mixed.

2 Rinse the pulp and form sheets as usual. A flecked paper will result.

PURE GRASS (C)

• *1 cup cut grass*
• *Water*

1 Cook the grass in water for one hour. Drain and rinse.

2 Lightly process the cooked grass in the blender for two to three seconds.

3 Rinse the pulp and form sheets as usual. Produces fragrant sheets of paper.

INDEX

Figures in italics indicate captions.

A

action designs (origami) 42–43
Aharoni, Gilad *15*
airmail paper 9
angle division (origami) 23
Ariel, Liat Binyamini: *Magic Pumpkins 137*
armatures (paper sculpture) 70–71
assembly (paper sculpture) 70

B

balloon base (origami) 31–32
Bar Am, Anat
  Greta (the Guardian Cat) 128
  Tamashi Birds 132
bases (origami) 26–34
Binzinger, Evi: *Blue Elephant 14*
bird base (origami) 28–29
Blackman, John: *Barrel Cactus 28*
blintz base (origami) 27
boat base (origami) 32–33
bone folder *14*
book base (origami) 27
bookbinding 8, 76–91
  adhesives 77
  binding materials 77
  concertina book project 90–91
  multisection binding 85–87
  papers 77
  preparing the book block 78–79
  single-section binding 82–84
  soft and hard covers 80–81
  stab binding 88–89
bookbinding awl *76*
boxes, pop-up 56–57
Brodskaya, Yulia
  Havas Annual Report 92
  Scent 93
Brown, Hannah
  Airplane 15
  Flying High 78
  Headlamp 76
  Out for a Walk 76
butterfly keepsake box (quilling) 98–101
butterfly (origami) 35

C

card-weight paper 8
cartridge paper 8, 9
collage 9, 120–127
  composition 124–125
  cutting and pasting 122–123
  history 121
  methods 121
  painted paper collage project 126–127
  papers 121
  tools *121*
concertina book project 90–91
cones (paper sculpture) 64–65
Coron, Béatrice
  Balloon City 112
  Sun City 114
couching 146, 147
creasing by hand 12
cupboard base (origami) 27
cut-score 13
cutting
  with a knife 13
  safe 13
  with scissors 13
cylinders (paper sculpture) 64, 65

D

Davidson, Ann
  Ceathramh Garbh, Ardmore, Sutherland 124
  A Gale in Strath Fleet, Sutherland 122
  Kylesku, Sutherland 120
  The Rocks of Loch Laxford, Sutherland 121
decorative designs (origami) 35–37
decorative forms (paper sculpture) 66–69
drawing paper 8

E

edge division (origami) 22–23
egg stand (origami) 38–39
embedding techniques (papermaking) 149–150, 154–155
embossing techniques (papermaking) 150, 155–156
equilateral triangle 24
etching papers 9

F

fine art paper 9
fish base (origami) 34
five-module antiprisms (origami) 40–41
flapping bird (origami) 42
Fletcher, Barbara: *Whimsical Fish Lamps 137*
flower base (origami) 30–31
folds, basic (origami) 18–21
functional designs (origami) 38–39

G

Gannon, Patrick: *The Golden Sea, It Has Teeth 113*
geometric divisions (origami) 22–25
giftwrap 8, 9, *15*
Golan, Miri: *Untitled 14*
gold leaf 135

H

handmade papers 8, 9, 10, 135
hexagon 24
hungry crow (origami) 43

I

incised pop-ups 46–51
inclusions (papermaking) 150, 155
indenting (origami) 13

decorative forms (paper sculpture) 66–69
drawing paper 8

inside reverse fold (origami) 19
Irises 25
Irsara, Irma
  Arrestarsi ai raggi notturni 139
  Esperienze di colore 138
  In rima ai duscinetti d'uutunno 136

J

Jackson, Ellen
  Passion 102
  Pink/Black Royale 103
  Surface Play 102
Jackson, Paul
  Doodle Weave 107
  The Encyclopedia of Origami and Papercraft 7
  Two Hands Twice 6
  Untitled 45
  Woven Pattern 106
Jedrzejewska, Joanna
  Creamy Bowl 129
  Parrots 128
Johnson, Paul, *Book 44*
junk mail 9

K

Kirschenbaum, Marc: *Rock Crab 26*
kite base (origami) 26

L

laminating (papermaking) 149, 154
leaflets 9
Lee, Bovey: *The Bird That Thinks It's a Plane 113*
lighting 69
Louie, Cecelia
  Dragonfly 92
  Heart 96

M

medium-weight papers 9
Miyajima, Noboru and Gilas Aharoni: *Cow 15*

modular designs (origami) 40–41
mold and deckle sets *142*, 143
Mukerji, Meenakshi: *Stella 40*
multipiece pop-ups 52–55

N
newspapers 9
Nightflight project (paper sculpture) 72–75
Nishinaka, Jeffrey
  Golden Gate Bridge 69
  Preserve 62

O
octagon (origami) 25
origami 14–43
  action designs 42–43
  bases 26–34
  basic folds 18–21
  decorative designs 35–37
  functional designs 38–39
  geometric divisions 22–25
  history of 15
  modular designs 40–41
  papers 8, 9, 15
  symbols 16–17
outside reverse fold (origami) 20

P
paper
  types 8–9
  weights 9
paper bowl project, woven 108–111
paper cutting 9, 112–119
  history 113
  paper-cut window hanging project 118–119
  papers 113
  techniques 114–117
paper grain 10–11
paper pulping 9, 136–141
  applications 140–141
  decoration 137
  methods 137
  papers *136*, 137
  preparing the pulp 138–139
paper sculpture 8, 62–75
  assembly and armatures 70–71

cones and cylinders 64–65
decorative forms 66–69
Nightflight project 72–75
papers *62*, 63
papermaking 9, 142–157
  decorative techniques 149–151
  history 143
  making the paper 146–147
  making pulp 144–145
  papers 143
  pressing and drying 148
  recipes 152–157
  special equipment *142*, 143
papier mâché 9, 128–135
  casting from a found mold 130–131
  decorative ideas 134–135
  finishes *128*
  history 129
  methods 129
  papers 129
  using other molds 132–133
Parker, Renée
  Drip 131
  Etruscan Spring 130
  Felix 134
paste brushes 76
photocopy paper 8, 9, 15
picture frame (origami) 39
pigmenting paper 145, 153–154
plain papers 8
polygons (origami) 24–25
pop-ups 8, 44–61
  boxes 56–57
  history 45
  incised 46–51
  methods 45
  multipiece 52–55
  papers 45
  pop-up spider project 58–61
preliminary base (origami) 27–28
pulp
  painting with 151, 156
  pigmentation 145
  plant 145, 157
  recycled 144

Q
quilling 9, 92–101
  applications 96–97
  butterfly keepsake box 98–101
  equipment 93
  history 93
  papers 93
  shapes 94–95

R
rabbit ear fold 20–21
recycled papers 9, 144, 152–153
Reimer-Epp, Heidi: *Molded Bowl 143*
Rizk, Anne: *Infinity Book 77*
rolling cylinders 11
Ross, John 92

S
Sawatzky, Kathy: *Notecards 143*
scoring (paper sculpture) 12, 66–68
scrapbooking papers 8, 15
sealing (papier mâché) 134
Shen, Philip: *Dish 23*
Shlian, Matthew
  Paper Scales 63
  Warped Stellation 63
shredded paper 136
Siliakus, Ingrid
  Abstract 62
  Elevation Terracotta 10
  Innerrings 64
  Reflection on Sagrada Familia 68
sink fold (origami) 21
snail (origami) 36–37
spider project, pop-up 58–61
squash fold (origami) 18–19
stab binding 88–89

T
tabbing (paper sculpture) 70
table decorations (origami) 38–39
Takacs, Erika
  Evolution 140
  Red Boots 136
textured surfaces 69
Thomas, Lizzie: *Hidden Summer 113*
tissue papers 9
translucent papers 9

V
valley and mountain folds (origami) 18
varnishes 134
vatman's tears (papermaking) 147

W
"washi" papers 8, 15
watercolor papers 8, 9
weaving 9, 102–111
  designs 104–7
  history 103
  methods 103
  papers *102*, 103
  woven paper bowl project 108–111
Westing, Jemma
  Invasive Species: The Lionfish! 45
  Seed in the Wind 44
Weston, Heather: *Carousel Book 77*
Willitts, Anne
  Bowl Selection 108
  Newspaper Vase 103
window hanging project, paper-cut 118–119
Winn, Nancy: *Hare 129*
writing paper 8, 9, 15

CREDITS

Quarto would like to thank the following artists for kindly supplying images for inclusion in this book:

Anat Taler-Bar Am p.128bl, 132 *www.woodyloo.etsy.com*

Ann Davidson p.120–121b, 122b, 124bl

Anne Rizk p.77bl

Anne Willitts p.103br, 108

Barbara Fletcher p.137t

Béatrice Coron p.112bl, 114bl

Bovey Lee p.113br

Cecelia Louie p.93br, 96b

Ellen Jackson p.102bl/br, 103bl

Erika Takacs p.136, 140 (sp) *www.erikatakacs.com*

Evi Binzinger p.14t *www.artrovertiert.de; photographer: Hubertus Schueler www.hubertus-schueler.de*

Gilad Aharoni p.15bl *www.giladorigami.com; designer: Miyajima Noboru*

Hannah Brown p.15br, 76bl/br, 78 *www.han-made.net*

Heather Weston p.77br

Heidi Reimer-Epp p.143br *www.botanicalpaperworks.com*

Ingrid Siliakus p.10, 62bl, 64bl, 68r *http://ingrid-siliakus.exto.org*

Irma Irsara p.136bl, 138b, 139b *www.oleary-irsara.com*

Jeffrey Nishinaka p.62br, 69b *www.jeffnishinaka.com*

Jemma Westing p.44br, 45br

Joanna Jedrzejewska p.128br, 129bl *www.papier-mache.eu*

John Blackman p.28

Kathy Sawatzky p.143bl

Liat Binyamini Ariel p.137 *www.liatart.com*

Lizzie Thomas p.112tr *http://lizziethomas.co.uk*

Marc Kirschenbaum p.26 *http://origami.home.pipeline.com*

Matthew Shlian p.63bl/br *www.mattshlian.com*

Miri Golan p.14b *photographer: Leonid Patrol-Kwitkowski, Eretz Israel Museum*

Nancy Winn p.129br *www.nancywinnsundawg.com*

Patrick Gannon p.113bl *www.pgannon.com*

Paul Jackson p.6, 45bl, 106bl, 107br *photographer p.6: Leonid Padrul-Kwitkowski, Eretz Israel Museum; photographer p45bl, 106bl, 107br: David Birch*

Paul Johnson p.44bl

Renée Parker p.130, 131, 134 *www.reneezanceart.com*

Yulia Brodskaya p.92bl, 93bl *www.artyulia.com; photographer: John Ross*

COMMISSIONED ARTISTS
Quarto would like the thank the following artists who supplied work specially for the revised edition of this book:

Ayako Brodek p.16–43
Ayako Brodek founded *OriCraft.com* to bring her origami work to a wider audience. Ayako is the author of *Origami Jewelry* (Kodansha America, 2007).

Jemma Westing p.58–61
Jemma Westing is an interactive book designer, working for a range of clients. To see more of her work, visit: *www.jemmawesting.com.*

Cecelia Louie p.92–101
Cecelia Louie's first love is paper. She is a graduate of Emily Carr College of Art and Design, Vancouver, BC. She works as a graphic designer and enjoys giving quilling a modern twist. To view more of her work, visit: *www.craftingcreatures.blogspot.com.*

Anne Willitts p.108–111
A dedicated maker, Anne Willitts has worked in a wide range of media, from spinning and weaving, through embroidery, to felting and papermaking. She continues to experiment both with textiles and paper, bringing together her accumulated interests in mixed media and 3D installations. To see more of Anne's work, visit her website: *www.annecreative.co.uk.*

Lizzie Thomas p.118–119
Lizzie Thomas is a paper artist particularly inspired by the use of paper in Japanese cultural and spiritual life. For commissions please visit: *www.lizziethomas.co.uk.*

Some of the material in this revised edition originally appeared in Paul Jackson's *Encyclopedia of Papercraft and Origami Techniques*, also published as *Artistry in Paper*.